INTRODUCING STRING DIAGRAMS

String diagrams are powerful graphical methods for reasoning in elementary category theory. Written in an informal expository style, this book provides a self-contained introduction to these diagrammatic techniques, ideal for graduate students and researchers. Much of the book is devoted to worked examples highlighting how best to use string diagrams to solve realistic problems in elementary category theory. A range of topics are explored from the perspective of string diagrams, including adjunctions, monad and comonads, Kleisli and Eilenberg–Moore categories, and endofunctor algebras and coalgebras. Careful attention is paid throughout to exploit the freedom of the graphical notation to draw diagrams that aid understanding and subsequent calculations. Each chapter contains plentiful exercises of varying levels of difficulty, suitable for self-study or for use by instructors.

RALF HINZE is Professor of Software Engineering at the University of Kaiserslautern-Landau (RPTU). His research is centered around the construction of provably correct software, with a particular emphasis on functional programming, algebra of programming, applied category theory, and persistent data structures. His goal is to develop theory, languages, and tools that simplify the construction of reliable software systems.

DAN MARSDEN is a theoretical computer scientist currently working as a Transitional Assistant Professor at the University of Nottingham. He is interested in the foundations of computer science, logic, and mathematics, with a particular emphasis on the application of category theory.

INTRODUCING STRING DIAGRAMS

The Art of Category Theory

RALF HINZE

University of Kaiserslautern-Landau

DAN MARSDEN

University of Nottingham

CAMBRIDGE
UNIVERSITY PRESS

Shaftesbury Road, Cambridge CB2 8EA, United Kingdom

One Liberty Plaza, 20th Floor, New York, NY 10006, USA

477 Williamstown Road, Port Melbourne, VIC 3207, Australia

314–321, 3rd Floor, Plot 3, Splendor Forum, Jasola District Centre, New Delhi – 110025, India

103 Penang Road, #05–06/07, Visioncrest Commercial, Singapore 238467

Cambridge University Press is part of Cambridge University Press & Assessment, a department of the University of Cambridge.

We share the University's mission to contribute to society through the pursuit of education, learning and research at the highest international levels of excellence.

www.cambridge.org
Information on this title: www.cambridge.org/9781009317863
DOI: 10.1017/9781009317825

First published 2023

A catalogue record for this publication is available from the British Library.

ISBN 978-1-009-31786-3 Hardback

Dedicated to Anja, Lisa, and Florian

Dedicated to Nuala, Florin, and Kiko

Contents

Prologue

Why should you read this book? Proofs in elementary category theory typically involve either the pasting together of commuting diagrams (Mac Lane, 1998) or calculational reasoning using chains of equalities (Fokkinga and Meertens, 1994). The first style is sometimes referred to as "diagram chasing" since the focus of a proof is chased around a diagram; the second is also known as "squiggoling" since it often involves the use of "squiggly" symbols.

Both styles have their merits. Commutative diagrams capture an abundance of type information, and invoke a certain amount of visual intuition. Equational proofs are familiar from many other branches of science and mathematics. They are also compact and carry a clear orientation from assumptions to goals.

Unfortunately, both styles also have serious limitations. The usual equational style of reasoning forces us to abandon the vital type information that guides proof attempts and protects against errors. Commuting-diagram-style proofs retain the type information. Sadly, the proof style is unfamiliar to many in other fields of mathematics and computer science, and the resulting proofs often lack motivation and a clear direction of argument. Further, much of the effort in these proofs can be consumed by trivial administrative steps involving functoriality, handling naturality componentwise, and the introduction and elimination of identities.

In order to recover the best of both these approaches, in this monograph we advocate the use of *string diagrams* (Penrose, 1971), a two-dimensional form of notation, which retains the vital type information while permitting an equational style of reasoning. The book can be seen as a graphical approach to elementary category theory, or dually as a course in string diagrammatic reasoning with elementary category theory as the running example.

The diagrammatic notation silently deals with distracting bookkeeping steps, such as naturality and functoriality issues, leaving us to concentrate on the essentials. This is an important aspect in any choice of notation, as advocated by Backhouse (1989). The resulting diagrams and proofs are highly visual and we can often exploit topological intuition to identify suitable steps in our reasoning. We aim to illustrate the efficiency and elegance of string diagrams with the many explicit calculations throughout the book.

There is a lack of expository material on the application of string diagrams. Probably the most substantial exception appears in the draft book (Curien, 2008a), and the shorter related conference paper (Curien, 2008b). These works are complementary to the current text, taking a rather different direction in their exploration of string diagrams. The standard introductory texts generally omit string diagrams, with the exception of a brief mention by Leinster (2014). This is unfortunate as it makes these beautiful methods unduly hard to pick up, without either access to experts, or detailed knowledge of the academic literature. This monograph aims to address this gap.

This is *not* a book on the mathematical foundations of string diagrams. Instead, it is a guide for users, with many explicit calculations illustrating how to apply string diagrams. The aesthetics of string diagrams are important; a bad drawing can become a baffling mass of spaghetti, whereas good diagrammatic choices can render proof steps almost embarrassingly obvious. We explore how to exploit this artistic freedom effectively throughout the text.

Can you read this book? We have aimed for a minimum of prerequisites for readers, beyond a certain level of mathematical maturity. Ideally, you should have some familiarity with the basic objects of discrete maths, such as preorders and partial orders, monoids, and graphs, at the level of Gries and Schneider (2013), for example.

Readers who have already been introduced to category theory will find much that is new, as our consistent use of string diagrams will shed new light on even familiar calculations. Those with more expertise, who are familiar with notions such as 2-categories, bicategories, and the ideas of formal category theory within them, will hopefully see applications well beyond our stated scope of elementary category theory.

How should you read this book? Chapter 1 introduces many preliminary categorical ideas and examples, laying foundations and fixing notation for later. Readers with some basic familiarity with category theory can probably skip this chapter, returning for details as necessary. String diagrams, the core subject of the book, are introduced in Chapter 2, along with some preliminary examples to start developing intuition for the notation. Chapters 3, 4, and 5 then explore the important topics of monads and adjunctions, using diagrammatic methods.

Along the way, further extensions and perspectives on the graphical notation are introduced and applied. The chapters are probably best read sequentially, as each builds upon the last, allowing us to steadily ramp up to richer examples.

Readers will find we put little emphasis on explicit lemmas and theorems in the text. Instead the focus is on *how* to prove things. As with any mathematics book, it is best read with an accompanying pen and paper, and we suggest that readers draw their own pictures and proofs as they follow along.

The end of each chapter contains a selection of supporting exercises. These have been carefully chosen to reinforce the ideas within the chapter, and readers are encouraged to solve at least the easier questions to check their understanding. To aid the selection of exercises we have made an attempt to indicate the difficulty level or time investment:

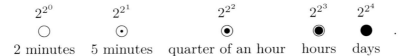

The scheme works on a superexponential scale, ranging from "drill" questions to topics for further research. Of course, the difficulty levels are highly subjective: what some find easy, poses a challenge to others.

In the intended sequel to this monograph, "Exploring String Diagrams— The Art of Category Theory," which we shall tersely refer to as ESD, we plan to delve further into the world of string diagrams. We shall occasionally make forward references to establish connections to ideas intended for ESD, but the current book can be read entirely independently.

How does this connect to applied category theory? Graphical languages are commonplace in applied category theory, with much interest stimulated by the categorical quantum mechanics program (Abramsky and Coecke, 2004).

Opening any textbook in mathematics or the sciences, one quickly encounters diagrams, for example many types of circuits or networks. In conventional texts, they do little more than furnish intuition. A theme of applied category theory is to take these diagrams more seriously, and to exploit them directly in calculations. There are many examples, including quantum theory (Coecke and Kissinger, 2017; Heunen and Vicary, 2019), natural language semantics (Coecke et al., 2010), signal flow graphs (Bonchi et al., 2015), control theory (Baez and Erbele, 2015), economic game theory (Ghani et al., 2018a,b), Markov processes (Baez et al., 2016), analogue (Baez and Fong, 2015) and digital (Ghica and Jung, 2016) electronics and hardware architecture (Brown and Hutton, 1994), machine learning (Fong et al., 2019), and linear algebra (Sobocinski, 2019).

Category theory is the underlying tool upon which all these concrete applications have been built. The current monograph brings graphical methods to bear upon category theory itself. Both users and developers of these diagrammatic languages will find new applications for their graphical intuitions, and hopefully it will also serve as a gateway into the myriad disciplines where graphical reasoning finds a home.

Genesis of the book. The use of string diagrams crept up gradually on the authors. The first author exploited string diagrams in connection to program optimization and monads (Hinze, 2012). At this point both conventional and graphical reasoning are developed in parallel, rather than making the jump to fully diagrammatic arguments.

Meanwhile, the second author was completing a DPhil. in the Quantum group at Oxford, a hotbed for diagrammatic reasoning, and was starting to find string diagrams indispensable for understanding aspects of monad theory. This eventually led to a preliminary account of string diagrammatic elementary category theory (Marsden, 2014, 2015).

Eventually, the two authors noted their common interests, and joined forces, after managing to agree on which way round the diagrams should be drawn! This collaboration led to two papers further fleshing out how effective diagrammatic reasoning can be for elementary category theory (Hinze and Marsden, 2016a,b). This was followed by practical teaching of these ideas by both authors, in the form of invited tutorials at the 21st Estonian Winter School in Computer Science, and QPL 2017.

Throughout this process the authors have learned much about how to best use string diagrams. Many diagrams have been tuned and adjusted to better exploit the notation, with early attempts by both authors being rather naive in their use of the topological freedom afforded by the notation. Eventually our minds, and diagrams, became more flexible as we properly absorbed the capabilities of string diagrams. As their eyes have become open, both authors have also been pleasantly surprised at the sheer breadth of situations in which string diagrammatic arguments prove effective. The current monograph captures our more mature understanding of how string diagrams can best be applied.

Acknowledgements. The authors would like to thank Samson Abramsky, Eugenia Cheng, Bob Coecke, Jeremy Gibbons, Chris Heunen, Markus Kurtz, Alexander Kurz, Dusko Pavlovic, David Reutter, Malte Schütze, Ross Street, Joshua Tan, Tarmo Uustalu, Jamie Vicary, Tobias Zimmermann, Maaike Zwart, and the members of Oxford Quantum Group for helpful discussions on various aspects of this work. We are grateful to the anonymous reviewer for their careful reading and detailed feedback on an earlier draft, and to Anna Scriven and David Tranah at Cambridge University Press for their support. We would also like to thank the audiences of the 21st Estonian Winter School in Computer Science, QPL 2017, and STRINGS 2017, for their feedback on various presentations of our ideas.

During this book's gestation, the second author has benefited from the support of an EPSRC DTG Grant, support from the Institute for Information and communications Technology Promotion (IITP) grant funded by the Korea government (MSIT) (No. 2015-0-00565, Development of Vulnerability Discovery Technologies for IoT Software Security), AFSOR grant "Algorithmic and Logical Aspects when Composing Meanings," and EPSRC grant "Resources and co-resources: a junction between categorical semantics and descriptive complexity."

Kaiserslautern, Ralf Hinze
Oxford, Dan Marsden

1

Category Theory

Elementary category theory is concerned with categories, functors, and natural transformations. As described in Mac Lane (1998):

"category" has been defined in order to be able to define "functor" and "functor" has been defined in order to be able to define "natural transformation."

We shall consider each notion in turn, whilst simultaneously preparing the grounds for string diagrams to be introduced in Chapter 2.

1.1 Categories

A *category* consists of objects and arrows between objects. The letters $\mathcal{C}$, $\mathcal{D}$, ... range over categories, and the uppercase letters A, B, ... over objects. We write $A : \mathcal{C}$ to express that A is an object of the category $\mathcal{C}$. Lowercase letters f, g, ... range over arrows, and we write $f : A \to B : \mathcal{C}$ to express that f is an arrow from A to B in the category $\mathcal{C}$. The object A is called the *source* of f and B its *target*. If $\mathcal{C}$ is obvious from the context, we abbreviate $f : A \to B : \mathcal{C}$ by $f : A \to B$.

For every object $A : \mathcal{C}$ there is an arrow $id_A : A \to A$, called the *identity*. Two arrows can be *composed* if their types match: if $f : A \to B$ and $g : B \to C$, then $g \cdot f : A \to C$ (pronounced "g after f"). We require composition to be unital and associative, with identity as its neutral element:

$$id_B \cdot f = f = f \cdot id_A, \tag{1.1a}$$
$$(h \cdot g) \cdot f = h \cdot (g \cdot f). \tag{1.1b}$$

1.1.1 Examples of Categories. To make the abstract notion of category more tangible, we introduce several examples, many of which will accompany us throughout the monograph. We begin with two trivial but useful categories:

Example 1.1 (**0** and **1**). There is a category, denoted **0**, with no objects and no arrows. There is also a category **1**, with one object and one arrow, the identity on the single object. □

Categories can be seen as generalizations of possibly more familiar mathematical objects.

Example 1.2 (Monoids and Preorders). Two extreme classes of categories are worth singling out.

A monoid $(A, e, \bullet)$ can be seen as a category that has exactly one object. The arrows are the elements of the monoid: e serves as the identity and $\bullet$ as composition.

A preorder $(A, \leqslant)$ can be seen as a category with at most one arrow between any two objects, which are the elements of the preorder. There exists an arrow of type $a \to b$ if and only if $a \leqslant b$; reflexivity ensures the existence of identities and transitivity the existence of composites. □

A category is often identified with its collection of objects: we loosely say that **Set** is the category of sets. However, equally if not more important are the arrows of a category. So, **Set** is really the category of sets and total functions. There is also **Rel**, the category of sets and relations.

Remark 1.3 (Preservation and Reflection of Structure). An arrow *preserves* structure if features of the source allow us to deduce features of the target. For example, if $h : (A, 0, +) \to (B, 1, \times)$ is a monoid homomorphism, and $a + a' = 0$ holds in the source monoid, then $h\,a \times h\,a' = 1$ holds in the target monoid. This is exactly the motivation for homomorphisms between algebraic structures: they *preserve equations*.

An arrow *reflects* structure if we can infer properties of the source from properties of the target. Notice the backward direction of travel.

To illustrate this, let us first establish some useful notation that we need time and again. For a function $f : A \to B$ there is a *direct image function* taking subsets of A to subsets of B:

$$f^\blacktriangleright X := \{\, y \in B \mid \exists x \in X \,.\, f\,x = y \,\}.$$

There is also an *inverse image function*, mapping subsets in the opposite direction:

$$f^\blacktriangleleft Y := \{\, x \in A \mid \exists y \in Y \,.\, f\,x = y \,\}.$$

With this notation in place, if $h : A \to B$ is a continuous map of topological spaces, $Y \subseteq B$ being an open subset of B implies $f^\blacktriangleleft Y \subseteq A$ is an open set in A. So, structure in the target implies structure in the source, and these topological arrows reflect structure. □

Example 1.4 (Sets and Structures). Many examples of categories used in practice are sets with additional structure, and functions that preserve or reflect this structure.

Sets with additional structure include monoids, groups, preorders, lattices, graphs, and so on. In each of these cases the arrows are structure-preserving maps. For example, **Mon** is the category of monoids and monoid homomorphisms. Notice the difference as compared to Example 1.2. There we considered a single monoid; here we consider the collection of all monoids and homomorphisms between them. Likewise, we can form the category **Pre**, whose objects are preorders and whose arrows are monotone or order-preserving functions.

Further examples include **Bool**, **Sup**, and **CompLat**, which are respectively the categories of Boolean lattices, complete join-semilattices, and complete lattices, with homomorphisms preserving the algebraic structure. Note that, although every complete join-semilattice is automatically a lattice, the categories **Sup** and **CompLat** are different, as the arrows preserve different structure.

As well as these examples with structure-preserving maps, there are examples where the arrows *reflect* structure, such as the categories **Top** and **Met** of topological spaces and metric spaces, with continuous maps as arrows. □

The following category, which will accompany us as a running example, is perhaps slightly more unusual.

Example 1.5 (Category of Actions). Let $(M, e, \bullet)$ be a fixed monoid. The objects of the category M-**Act** are pairs $(A, \lhd)$, where A is a set and $(\lhd) : M \times A \to A$ is an operation that respects the monoid structure:

$$e \lhd a = a, \tag{1.2a}$$

$$(m \bullet n) \lhd a = m \lhd (n \lhd a). \tag{1.2b}$$

The operation is also called a *left action of* M. An arrow $f : (A, \lhd) \to (B, \blacktriangleleft)$ in M-**Act** is a function of type $A \to B$ that preserves actions:

$$f (m \lhd a) = m \blacktriangleleft f a, \tag{1.3}$$

also known as an *equivariant function*. □

There are many ways of constructing new categories from old, as we will see in later sections. For now, we consider three useful cases.

Definition 1.6 (Subcategories). A *subcategory* $\mathcal{S}$ of a category $\mathcal{C}$ is a collection of some of the objects and some of the arrows of $\mathcal{C}$, such that identity and composition are preserved to ensure $\mathcal{S}$ constitutes a valid category. For example, **Set** is a subcategory of **Rel** as every function is a binary relation. Commutative monoids **CMon** and commutative, idempotent monoids **CIMon** form subcategories of **Mon**.

In a *full subcategory* the collection of arrows is maximal: if $f : A \to B : \mathcal{C}$ and $A, B : \mathcal{S}$, then $f : A \to B : \mathcal{S}$. The category **Fin** of finite sets and total functions is a full subcategory of **Set**.   ☐

Definition 1.7 (Opposite Categories). For any category $\mathcal{C}$ we can consider its *opposite category* $\mathcal{C}^{op}$. This has the same objects as $\mathcal{C}$, but an arrow of type $A \to B$ in $\mathcal{C}^{op}$ is an arrow of type $B \to A$ in $\mathcal{C}$. Identities in $\mathcal{C}^{op}$ are as in $\mathcal{C}$, and composition in $\mathcal{C}^{op}$ is given by forming the reverse composite in $\mathcal{C}$. The process of swapping source and target is purely bureaucratic; it does not do anything to the arrows.   ☐

Definition 1.8 (Product Categories). For any pair of categories $\mathcal{C}$ and $\mathcal{D}$ we can form their product $\mathcal{C} \times \mathcal{D}$. An object of the *product category* is a pair of objects (A, B) with $A : \mathcal{C}$ and $B : \mathcal{D}$; an arrow of type $(A, C) \to (B, D) :$ $\mathcal{C} \times \mathcal{D}$ is a pair of arrows (f, g) with $f : A \to B : \mathcal{C}$ and $g : C \to D : \mathcal{D}$. Identity and composition are defined componentwise,

$$id_{(A,B)} := (id_A, id_B), \tag{1.4a}$$

$$(g_1, g_2) \cdot (f_1, f_2) := (g_1 \cdot f_1, g_2 \cdot f_2), \tag{1.4b}$$

in terms of identity and composition of the underlying categories.   ☐

1.1.2 Graphical Representation of Objects and Arrows. We have noted in the prologue that notation matters, so a brief discussion of the syntax is certainly not amiss. Composition of arrows is a binary operation. Applications of binary operations or 2-ary functions are variably written prefix *op a b*, infix *a op b*, or postfix *a b op*, often with additional syntactic ornaments such as parentheses or commas. We have opted to write composition infix as $g \cdot f$. Why? Infix notation has a distinct advantage over the alternatives when expressions are nested as in $h \cdot g \cdot f$. At the outset, nested infix expressions are ambiguous, consider for example $a - b - c$. Do we intend to say $(a - b) - c$ or $a - (b - c)$? Convention has it that $a - b - c$ is resolved to $(a - b) - c$. For composition, however, the problem of ambiguity dissolves into thin air as composition is associative (1.1b). Here a bug has been turned into a feature: in calculations we do not have to invoke the associative law explicitly; it is built into the notation. By contrast, say we wrote composition prefix; then we are forced to express $h \cdot g \cdot f$ as either $comp\,(h, comp\,(g, f))$ or as $comp\,(comp\,(h, g), f)$. The syntax forces us to make an unwelcome distinction.

Composition of arrows in categories lends itself well to a graphical representation using vertices and edges. There are basically two options: objects can be represented by vertices, and arrows by edges between them, or vice versa:

$$
\begin{array}{cc}
\text{Objects} & \text{Arrows} \\
A & B \quad f \quad A \\
\bullet & \bullet\!\!-\!\!\!-\!\!\!-\!\!\bullet
\end{array}
\qquad \text{versus} \qquad
\begin{array}{cc}
\text{Objects} & \text{Arrows} \\
\underline{}\;A & \underline{B\;\; f\;\; A} \\
\end{array}
\quad .
$$

The two types of diagrams are related by *topological* or *Poincaré duality*, where vertices become edges and edges become vertices. There are many variations of the two schemes. Vertices are often drawn as boxes or are not drawn at all, being replaced by their labels. Edges are often directed to allow for a more flexible arrangement of vertices. We avoid arrowheads by agreeing that the flow is from *right to left*. This choice blends well with the symbolic notation in that the graphical direction of composition,

$$
\begin{array}{cccc}
h & g & f \\
\bullet\!-\!\bullet\!-\!\bullet\!-\!\bullet \\
D & C & B & A
\end{array}
\qquad
\begin{array}{cccc}
h & g & f \\
\underline{\bullet\;\;\bullet\;\;\bullet\;\;\bullet} \\
D & C & B & A
\end{array} ,
$$

follows the direction in the term $h \cdot g \cdot f$. For reasons of consistency, we should also write the types backwards: if $g : C \leftarrow B$ and $f : B \leftarrow A$, then $g \cdot f : C \leftarrow A$. We stick to the customary notation, however, and use right-to-left types only for emphasis. (An alternative is to change the order of composition: forward composition $f \,;\, g \,;\, h$ blends well with left-to-right types. We use both forward and backward composition.)

Like the symbolic notation, the diagrammatic representations have associativity (1.1b) built in, as we are simply threading beads on a necklace. We can further obviate the need for invoking unitality (1.1a) explicitly by agreeing that the identity arrow on an object A is represented by the rendition of A. The same convention is also used in symbolic notation: the identity on A is often written $A : A \to A$. A distinctive advantage of diagrams over terms is that they add vital type information. For a monoid $a \cdot b$ is always defined. However, as composition is in general partial, our notation should prevent us from joining arrows together incorrectly.

We have two graphical representations to choose from. But which one to pick? Different communities have different preferences: theoreticians seem to prefer the diagrams on the left above (e.g. as parts of commuting diagrams; see Section 1.7.2), while hardware people seem to prefer the diagrams on the right (e.g. in the form of circuit diagrams). We favor the latter notation for reasons that will become clear later.

1.2 Properties of Arrows

We now consider categorical generalizations of injective, surjective, and bijective functions.

1.2.1 Mono and Epi Arrows. An arrow $f : A \to B$ is called *mono* if it is *left-cancelable*:

$$f \cdot x_1 = f \cdot x_2 \implies x_1 = x_2, \tag{1.5a}$$

for all objects X and all arrows $x_1, x_2 : X \to A$. In **Set** these are the injective functions. Dually, an arrow $f : A \to B$ is called *epi* if it is *right-cancelable*:

$$x_1 \cdot f = x_2 \cdot f \implies x_1 = x_2, \tag{1.5b}$$

for all objects X and all arrows $x_1, x_2 : B \to X$. In **Set** these are the surjective functions. The inverse directions of the cancellation properties (1.5a) and (1.5b) are Leibniz's context rules,

$$x_1 = x_2 \implies f \cdot x_1 = f \cdot x_2, \tag{1.5c}$$
$$x_1 = x_2 \implies x_1 \cdot f = x_2 \cdot f, \tag{1.5d}$$

so implications (1.5a) and (1.5b) can both be strengthened to equivalences.

1.2.2 Split Mono and Split Epi Arrows. For an arrow $f : A \to B$, a *post-inverse* of f is an arrow $k : A \leftarrow B$ such that

$$k \cdot f = id_A.$$

In this case, f is referred to as a *split mono*. Dually, a *pre-inverse* of f is an arrow $h : A \leftarrow B$ such that

$$f \cdot h = id_B.$$

Such an f is referred to as a *split epi*.

In pictures, these are arrows that annihilate each other if they touch in the right order:

$$\frac{\overset{k}{\bullet}\ \overset{f}{\bullet}}{A\ \ B\ \ A} = \frac{}{A} \quad \text{and} \quad \frac{\overset{f}{\bullet}\ \overset{h}{\bullet}}{B\ \ A\ \ B} = \frac{}{B}.$$

Observe that the identity arrows are rendered by edges.

In **Set**, almost every injective function has a post-inverse. The only exceptions are functions of type $\emptyset \to A$ with $A \neq \emptyset$, simply because there are no functions of type $A \to \emptyset$. However, every surjective function has a pre-inverse.

Occasionally it is useful to reinterpret categorical notions using set-theoretic spectacles. If we partially apply the composition operator, $- \cdot f$ or $g \cdot -$, we obtain maps over collections of arrows. Using these maps we can reinterpret the notions of mono and epi. Property (1.5a) captures that $f \cdot -$ is injective; likewise, (1.5b) states that $- \cdot f$ is injective:

$$(f \cdot -)\, x_1 = (f \cdot -)\, x_2 \implies x_1 = x_2,$$
$$(- \cdot f)\, x_1 = (- \cdot f)\, x_2 \implies x_1 = x_2.$$

While cancellation properties are related to injectivity, existence of a pre- or a post-inverse are related to surjectivity:

$$g \cdot - \text{ injective} \iff g \text{ mono},\qquad\qquad\text{(1.6a)}$$
$$- \cdot f \text{ injective} \iff f \text{ epi},\qquad\qquad\text{(1.6b)}$$
$$g \cdot - \text{ surjective} \iff g \text{ split epi},\qquad\qquad\text{(1.6c)}$$
$$- \cdot f \text{ surjective} \iff f \text{ split mono}.\qquad\qquad\text{(1.6d)}$$

The proofs of (1.6c) and (1.6d) are relegated to Exercise 1.8. The preceding list of equivalences partially explains why there are four different notions, rather than only two as in **Set**.

1.2.3 Isomorphisms. Two objects A and B are isomorphic, written $A \cong B$, if there is a pair of functions $f : A \to B$ and $g : A \leftarrow B$ such that $f \cdot g = id_B$ and $id_A = g \cdot f$. If an arrow $f : A \to B$ has both a pre- and a post-inverse, then they coincide, and we denote them f°. In this case f is an *isomorphism*, *iso* for short, with *inverse* f°, written $f : A \cong B : f^\circ$:

$$\frac{\overset{f^\circ}{\bullet}\ \overset{f}{\bullet}}{A\quad B\quad A} = \frac{}{A} \quad \text{and} \quad \frac{\overset{f}{\bullet}\ \overset{f^\circ}{\bullet}}{B\quad A\quad B} = \frac{}{B}.$$

In **Set**, the isos are exactly the bijective functions.

The relation $\cong$ is an equivalence relation: it is reflexive, symmetric, and transitive. Furthermore, it is compatible with most constructions on objects. Reflexivity is established by identity arrows:

$$id_A : A \cong A : id_A.$$

Symmetry is shown by exchanging the isomorphisms:

$$f : A \cong B : f^\circ \implies f^\circ : B \cong A : f.$$

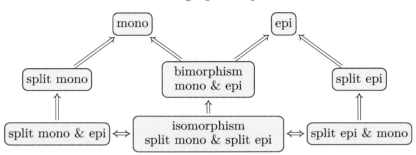

Figure 1.1 Properties of arrows.

Transitivity is established by suitably composing the witnesses:

$$f : A \cong B : f^\circ \;\land\; g : B \cong C : g^\circ \quad\Longrightarrow\quad g \cdot f : A \cong C : f^\circ \cdot g^\circ.$$

To prove that the composites are isomorphisms, we first annihilate the inner arrows and then the outer ones.

$$\frac{\overset{f^\circ}{}\;\overset{g^\circ}{}\;\overset{g}{}\;\overset{f}{}}{A \quad B \quad C \quad B \quad A} \;=\; \frac{\overset{f^\circ}{}\qquad\overset{f}{}}{A \quad B \quad A} \;=\; \frac{}{A}.$$

The proof for the reverse direction is entirely analogous.

Figure 1.1 relates the various properties of arrows – an *isomorphism* is an arrow that is both split mono and split epi; an arrow that is both mono and epi is called a *bimorphism*. The identity has all the properties, and all the properties are preserved by composition. Exercise 1.11 asks you to establish the relations and to show that the inclusions are proper.

The attentive reader may have noted that categorical concepts come in pairs. An epi in $\mathcal{C}$ is a mono in $\mathcal{C}^{\mathrm{op}}$; a split epi in $\mathcal{C}$ is a split mono in $\mathcal{C}^{\mathrm{op}}$; the concept of an iso is self-dual; an iso in $\mathcal{C}$ is an iso in $\mathcal{C}^{\mathrm{op}}$. Duality means that we get two concepts for the price of one. The next section provides further evidence for the economy of expression afforded by duality.

1.3 Thinking in Terms of Arrows

A category consists of objects and arrows. However, these entities are not treated on an equal footing: category theory puts the conceptual emphasis on arrows. Indeed, to master the subject one has to learn to think in terms of arrows. To illustrate, let us define some additional infrastructure: initial and final objects, products and coproducts, and exponentials. In each case, the defined object is characterized in terms of its relationship to other objects. In a sense, category theory is the most social of all mathematical foundations.

1.3.1 Initial and Final Objects. Let $\mathcal{C}$ be a category. An object $0 : \mathcal{C}$ is called *initial in* $\mathcal{C}$ if, for each object $A : \mathcal{C}$, there is exactly one arrow from the initial object 0 to A. This property is referred to as the *universal property* of initial objects.

Dually, $1 : \mathcal{C}$ is a *final* or *terminal object in* $\mathcal{C}$ if it satisfies the *universal property* that, for each object $A : \mathcal{C}$, there is a unique arrow from A to 1. A final object in $\mathcal{C}$ is an initial object in $\mathcal{C}^{\mathrm{op}}$.

An object that is simultaneously initial and final in $\mathcal{C}$ is called a *zero object*.

Example 1.9 (Preorders). An initial object in a preorder category is a least element. Dually, a final object is a greatest element. If the preorder is a partial order, meaning the relation $\leqslant$ is also antisymmetric, then initial and final objects are unique. □

Example 1.10 (Sets and Structures). In **Set**, the empty set is initial and *any* singleton set is final. In **Mon**, the singleton monoid $(\{()\}, (), \bullet)$ with $() \bullet () = ()$ is both initial and final, as homomorphisms have to preserve the neutral element: the singleton monoid is a zero object. □

The examples demonstrate that, in general, initial and final objects are not unique. They are, however, *unique up to a unique isomorphism*. If A and B are both initial, then there are unique arrows of type $A \to B$ and $B \to A$, whose compositions are necessarily identities.

1.3.2 Products and Coproducts. A *product* of two objects B_1 and B_2 consists of an object written as $B_1 \times B_2$ and a pair of *projection arrows*:

$$outl : B_1 \times B_2 \to B_1 \quad \text{and} \quad outr : B_1 \times B_2 \to B_2.$$

These three entities have to satisfy the following *universal property*: for each object A and for each pair of arrows $f_1 : A \to B_1$ and $f_2 : A \to B_2$, there exists an arrow $f_1 \vartriangle f_2 : A \to B_1 \times B_2$ (pronounced "f_1 *split* f_2") such that

$$f_1 = outl \cdot g \;\wedge\; f_2 = outr \cdot g \;\Longleftrightarrow\; f_1 \vartriangle f_2 = g, \tag{1.7}$$

for all $g : A \to B_1 \times B_2$. The equivalence captures the existence of an arrow satisfying the property on the left and furthermore states that $f_1 \vartriangle f_2$ is the *unique* such arrow. The following commutative diagram (see Section 1.7.2) summarizes the type information:

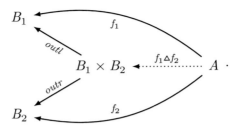

The dotted arrow indicates that $f_1 \vartriangle f_2$ is the unique arrow from A to $B_1 \times B_2$ that makes the diagram commute. Informally, the universal property states that for anything that "looks like" a product there is a unique arrow that factorizes the look-alike product in terms of a "real" product. Section 5.2 makes the notion of a universal construction precise.

The construction of products dualizes to coproducts, which are products in the opposite category. The *coproduct* of two objects A_1 and A_2 consists of an object written as $A_1 + A_2$ and a pair of *injection arrows*:

$$inl : A_1 \to A_1 + A_2 \quad \text{and} \quad inr : A_2 \to A_1 + A_2.$$

These three entities have to satisfy the following *universal property*: for each object B and for each pair of arrows $g_1 : A_1 \to B$ and $g_2 : A_2 \to B$, there exists an arrow $g_1 \triangledown g_2 : A_1 + A_2 \to B$ (pronounced "g_1 *join* g_2") such that

$$f = g_1 \triangledown g_2 \iff f \cdot inl = g_1 \ \wedge \ f \cdot inr = g_2, \tag{1.8}$$

for all $f : A_1 + A_2 \to B$. Reversing the arrows in the previous product diagram, we obtain the corresponding diagram for coproducts:

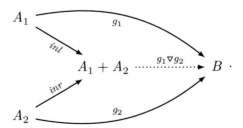

Remark 1.11 (Bigger Products and Coproducts). We have introduced binary products. Clearly, we can also define ternary products, with three projection arrows, and a corresponding universal property. These can be built by nesting binary products, with the order of composition unimportant, as

the two choices are isomorphic:

$$(X_1 \times X_2) \times X_3 \cong X_1 \times (X_2 \times X_3).$$

This game can be repeated to form the product of any finite collection of objects. As the notation will quickly become clumsy, we write the *indexed product* of an I-indexed family of objects $X_{i \in I}$ as $\prod_{i \in I} X_i$.

It is then natural to broaden things further, considering *infinite products*, where i ranges over an infinite set, although these cannot be formed by iterating the finite construction, and so a category with finite products may not have these larger ones. In general, we have a set of projection arrows, indexed by i, and for every family of arrows $f_i : A \to X_i$ a unique mediating arrow of type $A \to \prod_{i \in I} X_i$, generalizing $f_1 \vartriangle f_2$.

Dually, we can form *iterated*, potentially *infinite* coproducts, over some index set I; these will be denoted $\sum_{i \in I} X_i$. □

Example 1.12 (Preorders). In preorder categories, products are greatest lower bounds or meets, and coproducts are least upper bounds or joins. The *meet* of b_1 and b_2, written as $b_1 \sqcap b_2$, is defined by the equivalence

$$a \leqslant b_1 \ \wedge \ a \leqslant b_2 \iff a \leqslant b_1 \sqcap b_2. \tag{1.9a}$$

Dually, the *join* of a_1 and a_2, written $a_1 \sqcup a_2$, is defined by

$$a_1 \sqcup a_2 \leqslant b \iff a_1 \leqslant b \ \wedge \ a_2 \leqslant b. \tag{1.9b}$$

The uniqueness conditions are trivially satisfied as there is at most one arrow between any two objects. □

Example 1.13 (Sets). In the category of sets and total functions, the product is given by the Cartesian product:

$$B_1 \times B_2 := \{ (b_1, b_2) \mid b_1 \in B_1, b_2 \in B_2 \}.$$

The split operator and the projection functions are defined by

$$(f_1 \vartriangle f_2) \, a := (f_1 \, a, f_2 \, a) \qquad \text{and} \qquad \begin{aligned} outl \, (b_1, b_2) &:= b_1, \\ outr \, (b_1, b_2) &:= b_2. \end{aligned}$$

The coproduct corresponds to the *disjoint* union of sets:

$$A_1 + A_2 := \{ (0, a_1) \mid a_1 \in A_1 \} \cup \{ (1, a_2) \mid a_2 \in A_2 \}.$$

The injection functions and the join operator are defined by

$$\begin{aligned} inl \, a_1 &:= (0, a_1) \\ inr \, a_2 &:= (1, a_2) \end{aligned} \qquad \text{and} \qquad \begin{aligned} (g_1 \triangledown g_2) \, (0, a_1) &:= g_1 \, a_1, \\ (g_1 \triangledown g_2) \, (1, a_2) &:= g_2 \, a_2. \end{aligned}$$

The injection functions "tag" their arguments; the join operator performs a case analysis on the tag.

The category **Rel** has the same coproducts as **Set**. However, the products differ: as **Rel** is self-dual, coproducts and products coincide.   □

Observe that the duality of the "interfaces" – the universal properties (1.7) and (1.8) are like abstract interfaces – is not reflected in the "implementations" – the concrete definitions of the functions in **Set**. This leads to a second observation. A proof about products that is conducted in terms of the interface dualizes effortlessly to a proof about coproducts. A proof that is couched in terms of the concrete implementation is unlikely to enjoy the same reuse.

Like initial and final objects, products and coproducts are only defined up to isomorphism. (This statement can be sharpened, see Exercise 1.14.)

1.3.3 Exponentials. The *exponential* of two objects X and B in a category with products consists of an object written B^X and an arrow *apply* : $B^X \times X \to B$. These two entities have to satisfy the following *universal property*: for each object A and for each arrow $f : A \times X \to B$ there exists an arrow $\Lambda f : A \to B^X$ (pronounced "*curry f*") such that

$$f = apply \cdot (g \times id_X) \quad \Longleftrightarrow \quad \Lambda f = g, \tag{1.10}$$

for all $g : A \to B^X$. The product of arrows is defined $h \times k := (h \cdot outl) \vartriangle (k \cdot outr)$, see also Example 1.19. Like for products, the equivalence captures the existence of an arrow satisfying the property on the left and furthermore states that Λf is the *unique* such arrow, as shown in the following diagram:

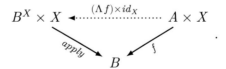

Example 1.14 (Preorders). In a Boolean lattice the exponential b^x is given by $b \sqcup \neg x$. It satisfies the following equivalence:

$$a \sqcap x \leqslant b \quad \Longleftrightarrow \quad a \leqslant b \sqcup \neg x.$$

In the smallest, nontrivial Boolean lattice $\mathbb{B}$, the exponential is often written as an implication: $b \Leftarrow x := b \sqcup \neg x$.   □

Example 1.15 (Sets). In **Set**, the exponential B^X amounts to the set of total functions from X to B. The operation Λ turns a two-argument function into a so-called curried function, a single-argument function of the first parameter that yields another single-argument function, which receives the second parameter. □

1.4 Functors

Every worthwhile algebraic *structure* comes equipped with corresponding *structure*-preserving maps; so do categories, where these maps are called *functors*. We let F, G, … range over functors. Since a category consists of two parts, objects and arrows, a functor $F : \mathcal{C} \to \mathcal{D}$ consists of a mapping on objects and a mapping on arrows, called the *object map* and the *arrow map* respectively. It is common practice to denote both maps by the same symbol. The two parts of a functor have to be consistent; for one thing, the action on arrows has to respect the types: if $f : A \to B : \mathcal{C}$, then $F f : F A \to F B : \mathcal{D}$. Furthermore, a functor has to preserve identities and composition:

$$F (id_A) = id_{F A}, \tag{1.11a}$$
$$F (g \cdot f) = F g \cdot F f. \tag{1.11b}$$

These are called the *functor laws*. Equation (1.11a) is the *functor identity law*, and Equation (1.11b) is the *functor composition law*.

A simple example of a functor is the *identity* $Id_\mathcal{C} : \mathcal{C} \to \mathcal{C}$, defined as

$$Id_\mathcal{C} A := A,$$
$$Id_\mathcal{C} f := f.$$

Functoriality is preserved under composition: given two functors $F : \mathcal{C} \to \mathcal{D}$ and $G : \mathcal{D} \to \mathcal{E}$, their *composite* $G{\circ}F : \mathcal{C} \to \mathcal{E}$ is defined as

$$(G{\circ}F) A := G (F A),$$
$$(G{\circ}F) f := G (F f).$$

Categories and functors between them themselves form a category, called **Cat**. To avoid paradoxes similar to Russell's paradox, this construction is subject to size constraints, see I.6 of Mac Lane (1998).

We will revisit functor composition in Section 2.1.

1.4.1 Examples of Functors. As we did with categories, we now consider some examples of functors to make things more concrete.

Example 1.16 (Functors between Monoids and Preorders)**.** We saw in Example 1.2 that monoids and preorders can be seen as categories. A functor between monoid categories is a monoid homomorphism; a functor between preorder categories is a monotone function. So, in this case, functors are the usual notion of homomorphism.   □

Example 1.17 (Functors from **0**, and to **1**). In Example 1.1 we introduced the empty category **0**. This category has the special property that there is exactly one functor to any category from **0**, as there is no data to specify. Similarly, the one object category **1** has the special property that there is exactly one functor from any category to **1**, as there is only one choice for where to send every object and arrow. In other words, **0** is the initial object in **Cat** and **1** is the final object.   □

Example 1.18 (Functors from and to Product Categories). A product category comes equipped with two projection functors, $\mathsf{Outl} : \mathcal{C}_1 \times \mathcal{C}_2 \to \mathcal{C}_1$ and $\mathsf{Outr} : \mathcal{C}_1 \times \mathcal{C}_2 \to \mathcal{C}_2$, defined as $\mathsf{Outl}\,(A_1, A_2) := A_1$, $\mathsf{Outl}\,(f_1, f_2) := f_1$ and $\mathsf{Outr}\,(A_1, A_2) := A_2$, $\mathsf{Outr}\,(f_1, f_2) := f_2$. A functor from a product category such as Outl and Outr is sometimes called a *bifunctor*, a contraction of the more unwieldy term *binary functor* (see also Exercise 1.23).

The *diagonal functor* $\Delta : \mathcal{C} \to \mathcal{C} \times \mathcal{C}$ is an example of a functor into a product category. It duplicates its argument:

$$\Delta\,A := (A, A), \tag{1.12a}$$
$$\Delta\,f := (f, f). \tag{1.12b}$$

We have $\mathsf{Outl} \circ \Delta = \mathsf{Id}_{\mathcal{C}_1}$ and $\mathsf{Outr} \circ \Delta = \mathsf{Id}_{\mathcal{C}_2}$.   □

Example 1.19 (Products and Exponentials). If the product $B_1 \times B_2$ exists for every pair of objects, $- \times =$ can be turned into a bifunctor with arrow map:

$$g_1 \times g_2 = (g_1 \cdot outl) \,\Delta\, (g_2 \cdot outr).$$

Likewise, if the exponential B^X exists for every object B, $(-)^X$ can be turned into a functor with arrow map:

$$f^X = \Lambda\,(f \cdot apply).$$

Exercise 1.24 asks you to fill in the details.   □

Many common mathematical constructions are functorial.

Example 1.20 (Powerset). Given a set A, we can form its powerset $\mathcal{P}\,A$ consisting of all subsets of A. This extends to a functor $\mathsf{Pow} : \mathbf{Set} \to \mathbf{Set}$, referred to as the *covariant powerset functor*, with action on arrows:

$$\mathsf{Pow}\,f := f^{\blacktriangleright}.$$

In fact, still taking the powerset construction on objects, we can extend this in a second way to a functor $2^{(-)} : \mathbf{Set}^{op} \to \mathbf{Set}$:

$$2^f := f^{\blacktriangleleft}.$$

This is referred to as the *contravariant powerset functor*, as it reverses the direction of arrows: $2^{g \cdot f} = 2^f \cdot 2^g$. The notation is inspired by the notation for exponentials: if we represent a set $X : \mathcal{P} A$ by its characteristic function $\chi : A \to 2$, then the action on arrows reads $2^f \psi = \psi \cdot f$, and consequently $2^f (2^g \psi) = 2^f (\psi \cdot g) = \psi \cdot g \cdot f = 2^{g \cdot f} \psi$. $\qquad \square$

The relationships between categories are important, and functors allow us to describe these relationships by showing how one can be transformed into the other.

Example 1.21 (Algebra and Order Theory)**.** A bounded join-semilattice is a partially ordered set with a bottom element, denoted $\bot$, and such that every pair of elements x, y has a least upper bound, or join, denoted $x \sqcup y$ (see Example 1.12).

Every commutative, idempotent monoid gives rise to a bounded join-semilattice, with order defined by $x \leqslant y \Longleftrightarrow x \bullet y = y$. The construction is functorial, as we can define:

$$\mathsf{Ord}\,(A, e, \bullet) := (A, \leqslant) \quad \textbf{where} \quad x \leqslant y \Longleftrightarrow x \bullet y = y,$$
$$\mathsf{Ord}\,h := h.$$

Conversely, given a bounded join-semilattice, we can define a commutative, idempotent monoid functorially, with the monoid operations given by the bottom element and joins:

$$\mathsf{CIMon}\,(A, \leqslant) := (A, \bot, \sqcup),$$
$$\mathsf{CIMon}\,h := h.$$

In fact, $\mathsf{Ord} \circ \mathsf{CIMon} = \mathsf{Id}$ and $\mathsf{CIMon} \circ \mathsf{Ord} = \mathsf{Id}$, so these constructions are inverse to each other, and we say that the categories of commutative, idempotent monoids and bounded join-semilattices are isomorphic. $\qquad \square$

For many functors there are often natural ways to travel back in the opposite direction. We return to monoids for an instructive example.

Example 1.22 (Free and Forgetful)**.** The category **Mon** is based on the category **Set** by adding more structure. This informal statement can be made precise via a functor. The *underlying* or *forgetful functor* $\mathsf{U} : \mathbf{Mon} \to$

Set is defined as

$$\mathsf{U}\,(A, e, \bullet) := A,$$
$$\mathsf{U}\,h := h. \tag{1.13}$$

The definition uses the fact that arrows in **Mon** are total functions. Since the action on arrows is the identity, the functoriality requirements are trivially satisfied.

The functor U has a counterpart, which takes an arbitrary set to the free monoid on the set. For that reason it is called the *free functor* $\mathsf{Free} : \mathbf{Set} \to \mathbf{Mon}$ and is defined as

$$\mathsf{Free}\,A := (A^*, [\,], +\!\!+),$$

$$\mathsf{Free}\,f := h\,\mathbf{where} \begin{cases} h\,[\,] := [\,], \\ h\,[\,a\,] := [f\,a], \\ h\,(x +\!\!+ y) := h\,x +\!\!+ h\,y. \end{cases}$$

Here, A^* is the set of all finite lists, whose elements are drawn from A. Lists can be constructed in three different ways: $[\,]$ is notation for the empty list, $[a]$ for the singleton list containing a, and $+\!\!+$ concatenates two lists. Concatenation is associative with $[\,]$ as its neutral element, so $(A^*, [\,], +\!\!+)$ is indeed a monoid. Furthermore, $\mathsf{Free}\,f$ is a monoid homomorphism by definition. It applies f to every element of a given list.

Composing the two functors gives an endofunctor on **Set**, which we call $\mathsf{List} := \mathsf{U} \circ \mathsf{Free} : \mathbf{Set} \to \mathbf{Set}$. The prefix "endo" emphasizes that source and target category of the functor are identical.   □

Example 1.23 (Polynomial Functors). A useful class of functors that commonly occur in practice are the *polynomial functors* on **Set**. These are functors built out of the iterated coproducts described in Remark 1.11, and exponentials. A polynomial functor is a functor of the following form:

$$X \mapsto \sum_{i \in I} X^{A_i}.$$

Here, the A_i are fixed sets. If we think of coproducts and exponentials as adding and raising to powers, the analogy with polynomials is clear.

Clearly the identity functor, $X \mapsto X^2$, and $X \mapsto X + X$ are examples of polynomial functors. Perhaps more surprisingly, the functor List of Example 1.22 is isomorphic to the polynomial functor:

$$X \mapsto \sum_{n \in \mathbb{N}} X^n.$$

As X^n is a tuple of n elements, our polynomial functor contains tuples of all potential lengths, exactly capturing lists of elements of X. □

One of the great strengths of category theory is its ability to build bridges between different areas of mathematics and computer science. The following miniature example points in that direction.

Example 1.24 (Category of Actions). Recall that a monoid $(M, e, \bullet)$ can be seen as a category $\mathcal{M}$. A functor $\mathcal{M} \to \mathbf{Set}$ is morally the same as an action of M; see Example 1.5. Since a monoid category has exactly one object, F selects a set and sends the monoid elements to endofunctions over that set. The coherence conditions for actions (1.2a) and (1.2b) correspond to the two functor laws. □

1.4.2 Graphical Representation of Functors. Let us extend the graphical representation of objects and arrows to functors. The coherence of the object and arrow maps and the functor laws allow us to push applications of functors inwards. Thus, a simple but slightly unimaginative approach is to label diagrams with functor applications:

$$\frac{\mathsf{F}\,h \quad \mathsf{F}\,g \quad \mathsf{F}\,f}{\mathsf{F}\,D \quad \mathsf{F}\,C \quad \mathsf{F}\,B \quad \mathsf{F}\,A}.$$

One could argue that the use of complex terms as labels mixes symbolic and diagrammatic notation. A more attractive alternative is to draw the functor as a separate wire extending diagrams to two dimensions. The application of a functor F to an object A and to an arrow f is rendered:

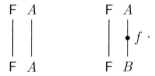

For reasons to become clear in Chapter 2, we have additionally rotated the diagrams 90° counterclockwise. We have also moved the labels to the ends of the wires to avoid cluttering the middle of the diagram.

Quite pleasingly, the functor laws are built into the notation, in the sense that equal terms have the same diagrams. Both sides of the identity functor law (1.11a) have the same depiction (1.14a). Similarly, both sides of the functor composition law (1.11b) correspond to diagram (1.14b):

(1.14a)   (1.14b)

Diagram (1.14b) can be divided into four parts as follows:

The functor composition law (1.11b) implies that it does not matter whether we assemble the parts first horizontally and then vertically, or vice versa.

1.5 Natural Transformations

Category theorists never study objects in isolation; they always consider what the right arrows between those objects should be. To this end, in Section 1.4 we introduced functors as the arrows between categories. As we have now introduced functors, we can play this game again. We should ask ourselves, what should the arrows between functors be? Answering this question leads to the definition of *natural transformations*. Before getting into the formal bureaucracy, we start with an example.

Consider the function that maps an element to a singleton list, $a \mapsto [a]$, and observe that the definition does not depend in any way on the nature of the element a. In particular, the map works uniformly across all possible *element types*. This characteristic can be made precise using the notion of a natural transformation.

Let $\mathsf{F}, \mathsf{G} : \mathcal{C} \to \mathcal{D}$ be two functors. A *transformation* $\alpha : \mathsf{F} \to \mathsf{G} : \mathcal{C} \to \mathcal{D}$ is a family of arrows, so that for each object $A : \mathcal{C}$ there is an arrow $\alpha A : \mathsf{F} A \to \mathsf{G} A : \mathcal{D}$. The arrow αA is called a *component* of α. A transformation can be seen as a map from objects to arrows.

A transformation is *natural*, written $\alpha : \mathsf{F} \dot{\to} \mathsf{G} : \mathcal{C} \to \mathcal{D}$, if

$$\mathsf{G}\, h \cdot \alpha X = \alpha Y \cdot \mathsf{F}\, h, \qquad (1.15)$$

for all arrows $h : X \to Y : \mathcal{C}$. Given α and h, there are essentially two ways of turning $\mathsf{F} X$ entities into $\mathsf{G} Y$ entities. The *naturality condition* demands that they are equal. We let α, β, ... range over natural transformations.

Condition (1.15) is equivalent to requiring commutativity of the following diagram:

$$
\begin{array}{ccc}
\mathsf{G}\,X & \xleftarrow{\ \alpha\,X\ } & \mathsf{F}\,X \\
{\scriptstyle \mathsf{G}\,h}\downarrow & & \downarrow{\scriptstyle \mathsf{F}\,h}\ . \\
\mathsf{G}\,Y & \xleftarrow[\ \alpha\,Y\ ]{} & \mathsf{F}\,Y
\end{array}
$$

Such a diagram is termed a *naturality square*.

As always, it is important to consider identities and composition. For any functor $\mathsf{F} : \mathcal{C} \to \mathcal{D}$ the identity arrows $id_{\mathsf{F}\,X} : \mathsf{F}\,X \to \mathsf{F}\,X$ form an *identity natural transformation* of type $\mathsf{F} \dot{\to} \mathsf{F}$,

$$
id_{\mathsf{F}}\,X := id_{\mathsf{F}\,X},
$$

with the naturality condition becoming trivial. Given three parallel functors $\mathsf{F}, \mathsf{G}, \mathsf{H} : \mathcal{C} \to \mathcal{D}$ and natural transformations $\alpha : \mathsf{F} \dot{\to} \mathsf{G}$ and $\beta : \mathsf{G} \dot{\to} \mathsf{H}$, we can form their *vertical composite* $\beta \cdot \alpha$ with components

$$
(\beta \cdot \alpha)\,X := \beta\,X \cdot \alpha\,X.
$$

The naturality condition follows immediately from the naturality of the two components. For fixed categories $\mathcal{C}$ and $\mathcal{D}$, functors of type $\mathcal{C} \to \mathcal{D}$ and natural transformations between these functors form a category, the *functor category* $\mathcal{D}^{\mathcal{C}}$.

Remark 1.25. We have seen product categories in Definition 1.8. In fact, they are the categorical products in **Cat**, and functor categories are the corresponding exponentials. This is a way of seeing that natural transformations are the right choice of arrows between functors. $\square$

We will revisit composition of natural transformations in Section 2.2. In particular, we shall see that there are also horizontal composites, and that the terms "vertical" and "horizontal" correspond to the graphical depiction of these different forms of composition.

1.5.1 Examples of Natural Transformations. As with the other members of the trinity of categorical concepts, we consider explicit examples of natural transformations. We begin with our usual favorites.

Example 1.26 (Monoid and Preorder Naturality). For monoids, a natural transformation between monoid homomorphisms $f, g : X \to Y$ is an element α of Y such that $g\,x \cdot \alpha = \alpha \cdot f\,x$. That is, the two homomorphisms are related pointwise by conjugation by the element α.

We saw that functors between preorders are monotone functions. In this special case there can be at most one natural transformation between such functors. In fact, for $f, g : X \to Y$ there is a natural transformation $f \mathbin{\dot\to} g$ if and only if $f\, x \leqslant g\, x$ for all $x \in X$. That is, if f is below g pointwise: $f \leqslant g$. The naturality condition is trivially satisfied as there is at most one arrow between any two objects. □

When categories are specialized to preorders, coherence conditions such as (1.15) are often vacuous. Turning things around, category theory can be seen as *order theory with coherence conditions* (Backhouse et al., 1998). An "order" between two objects, say A and B, is *witnessed* by one or more arrows of type $A \to B$. The coherence conditions ensure that the choice of the witness is compatible with the basic operations of category theory, identifying witnesses if necessary.

We saw in Example 1.20 that the powerset construction is functorial. Many operations on subsets are natural.

Example 1.27 (Operations on Sets)**.** The singleton set functions,

$$single\, A\, a := \{\, a\, \},$$

form a natural transformation $single : \mathsf{Id} \mathbin{\dot\to} \mathsf{Pow}$. The naturality condition $\mathsf{Pow}\, f \cdot single\, A = single\, B \cdot f$ holds by definition. Similarly, taking unions gives a natural transformation $\bigcup : \mathsf{Pow}\circ\mathsf{Pow} \mathbin{\dot\to} \mathsf{Pow}$. □

Many common computational tasks are natural.

Example 1.28 (Reducing Lists)**.** For each monoid $(A, e, \bullet)$ there is a monoid homomorphism, which reduces a list to a single element of A:

$$reduce\, (A, e, \bullet) := h \;\mathbf{where} \begin{cases} h\, [\,] := e, \\ h\, [a] := a, \\ h\, (x \mathbin{+\!\!+} y) := h\, x \bullet h\, y. \end{cases}$$

Instantiating the monoid to $(\mathbb{N}, 0, +)$, it sums a list of natural numbers. For $(\mathbb{B}, true, \wedge)$ it forms the conjunction of a list of Booleans. Its type is $\mathsf{Free}\, A \to (A, e, \bullet)$, which is equivalent to $\mathsf{Free}\, (\mathsf{U}\, (A, e, \bullet)) \to (A, e, \bullet)$. And, indeed, *reduce* is natural in the monoid $(A, e, \bullet)$, that is, $reduce : \mathsf{Free}\circ\mathsf{U} \mathbin{\dot\to} \mathsf{Id}$. Given $h : (A, 0, +) \to (B, 1, \times)$, the naturality condition is

$$h \cdot reduce\, (A, 0, +) = reduce\, (B, 1, \times) \cdot \mathsf{Free}\, (\mathsf{U}\, h).$$

This says that reducing a list using monoid A and then converting it to monoid B using h is the same thing as converting all the elements of the list to B using h, and then reducing the list using monoid B.

An application of *reduce* worth singling out is *join*, which flattens a list of lists of elements (recall that List = U∘Free):

$$join\ A := U\ (reduce\ (\textsf{Free}\ A)) : U\ (\textsf{Free}\ (U\ (\textsf{Free}\ A))) \to U\ (\textsf{Free}\ A).$$

The function is natural in A, that is, $join : \textsf{List}\circ\textsf{List} \overset{\cdot}{\to} \textsf{List}$. □

Example 1.29 (Category of Actions)**.** Continuing Example 1.24, a natural transformation between functors of type $\mathcal{M} \to \mathbf{Set}$ is morally the same as an equivariant map; see Example 1.5. The coherence condition (1.3) corresponds to the naturality square (1.15). Overall, the category $M\text{-}\mathbf{Act}$ of actions is isomorphic to the functor category $\mathbf{Set}^{\mathcal{M}}$. □

Example 1.30 (Nonnatural Transformation)**.** We have observed in the introduction that forming a singleton list is a natural transformation of type $\textsf{Id} \overset{\cdot}{\to} \textsf{List}$. There is, however, no natural transformation of type $\textsf{List} \overset{\cdot}{\to} \textsf{Id}$, as there is no *natural* way to define the image of the empty list. In a sense, we have to invent an element of the target type. This cannot be done uniformly – for the target type 0 this is even impossible. □

1.5.2 Graphical Representation of Natural Transformations. Turning to the graphical representation, we depict the component $\alpha\ A$ of a natural transformation, as on the left in the following diagram:

The diagrams for $\alpha\ A$ and $\textsf{F}f$ exhibit a nice symmetry: both consist of two parallel lines, one of which has a "bead" on it. We have noted above that the graphical notation silently deals with applications of the functor laws. The same holds true of the naturality condition (1.15) if we agree that diagrams that differ only in the relative vertical position of "beads," arrows and natural transformations, are identified:

(1.16)

This convention is a natural one, as the two strings are drawn in parallel, suggesting that the corresponding actions are independent of each other.

1.6 Properties of Functors

Like for arrows, we now consider categorical generalizations of injective, surjective, and bijective functions.

Since a functor is an arrow in **Cat**, it can be a (split) mono or a (split) epi. However, often weaker properties are more useful. Recall that a functor $F : \mathcal{C} \to \mathcal{D}$ consists of an object and an arrow map. If the former is injective (surjective), then F is said to be *injective* (*surjective*) *on objects*. If the latter is injective (surjective), then F is said to be *injective* (*surjective*) *on arrows*.

Two objects that exhibit exactly the same relationships cannot be distinguished: they are isomorphic. Isomorphism is a better notion of "sameness" for objects, rather than equality. The categorically natural properties of objects, such as being a terminal object, a product, or an exponential, are carried across isomorphisms. Consequently, we obtain more appropriate notions of "injective (surjective) on objects" if we replace equality by isomorphism.

1.6.1 Essentially Injective and Surjective Functors.
A functor $F : \mathcal{C} \to \mathcal{D}$ is *essentially injective* (on objects) if

$$F X_1 \cong F X_2 \implies X_1 \cong X_2, \tag{1.17a}$$

for all objects $X_1, X_2 : \mathcal{C}$.

A functor $F : \mathcal{C} \to \mathcal{D}$ is called *essentially surjective* (on objects) if

$$\forall B : \mathcal{D} . \exists A : \mathcal{C} . B \cong F A. \tag{1.17b}$$

A functor is *essentially bijective* if it is both essentially injective and essentially surjective.

1.6.2 Faithful and Full Functors.
While the object map of a functor is a single map, the arrow map is really a family of maps:

$$F_{A,B} : (A \to B : \mathcal{C}) \to (F A \to F B : \mathcal{D}),$$

with one member for each pair of objects. In fact, these maps are natural in both A and B, meaning that the following equation holds:

$$F k \cdot F_{A,B} f \cdot F h = F_{A',B'} (k \cdot f \cdot h),$$

which is an immediate consequence of the second functor law.

The functor F is *faithful* (*full*) if each of these maps is injective (surjective):

$$F \text{ faithful} \iff F_{A,B} \text{ injective for all } A \text{ and } B, \tag{1.18a}$$
$$F \text{ full} \iff F_{A,B} \text{ surjective for all } A \text{ and } B. \tag{1.18b}$$

A functor that is injective on arrows is also faithful, but not necessarily the other way round; see Exercise 1.31. For a subcategory $\mathcal{S}$ of $\mathcal{C}$, the inclusion functor $\mathcal{S} \to \mathcal{C}$ is both faithful and injective on objects. It is furthermore full if and only if $\mathcal{S}$ is a full subcategory.

For a functor that is *fully faithful* (full and faithful), the maps $\mathsf{F}_{A,B}$ form a natural bijection:

$$A \to B \quad \cong \quad \mathsf{F}\,A \to \mathsf{F}\,B. \tag{1.19}$$

A functor preserves isomorphisms; a fully faithful functor also reflects isomorphisms:

$$A \cong B \quad \Longleftrightarrow \quad \mathsf{F}\,A \cong \mathsf{F}\,B. \tag{1.20}$$

In other words, a fully faithful functor is essentially injective on objects.

1.7 Equational Reasoning

Category theory is essentially an algebraic theory: propositions take the form of equations, whose proofs are conducted using equational reasoning. Equational proofs are attractive for several reasons. First and foremost they are simple in the sense that they do not involve a lot of machinery – the basic step is to replace equals by equals. To establish $f = g$ one seeks intermediate terms h_0, ..., h_n such that $f = h_0 = \cdots = h_n = g$.

1.7.1 Symbolic Calculational Proofs. The following proof format, attributed to Wim Feijen (Gasteren, van, 1988, p. 107), is used throughout the monograph:

$$term_1$$
$$= \quad \{ \text{ hint 1 } \}$$
$$term_2$$
$$= \quad \{ \text{ hint 2 } \}$$
$$term_3.$$

Each step of the calculation is justified by a hint, enclosed in curly braces. The hints should enable the reader to easily verify that the calculation constitutes a valid proof.

It is instructive to work through a concrete example. (We will revisit the example in Section 2.4.1 once our graphical calculus is in place. Section 3.5 generalizes the example to a more abstract setting.) A common list-processing function is *filter* p : List $A \to$ List A, which takes a list as an argument and returns the list of all those elements, in order, that satisfy the predicate $p : A \to \mathbb{B}$. It is defined as

$$filter\, p := join\, A \cdot \mathsf{List}\, (guard\, p), \tag{1.21}$$

where $guard\, p : A \to \mathsf{List}\, A$ takes an element to a singleton list, if the element satisfies p, or to the empty list otherwise.

Our goal is to show that *filter* satisfies the following property:

$$filter\, p \cdot join\, A = join\, A \cdot \mathsf{List}\, (filter\, p), \tag{1.22}$$

for all objects A and for all arrows $p : A \to \mathbb{B}$. The equation can be paraphrased as follows: given a list of lists it does not matter whether we first flatten the lists and then filter the result, or we first filter the element lists individually and then flatten the filtered lists.

For the proof of (1.22) we need a fundamental property of flattening:

$$join\, A \cdot \mathsf{List}\, (join\, A) = join\, A \cdot join\, (\mathsf{List}\, A), \tag{1.23}$$

which states that the two ways of flattening a list of lists of lists of elements (a cubed list) are equivalent. We reason,

$$
\begin{aligned}
&filter\, p \cdot join\, A \\
=\ & \{\ \text{definition of } filter\ (1.21)\ \} \\
&join\, A \cdot \mathsf{List}\, (guard\, p) \cdot join\, A \\
=\ & \{\ join \text{ is natural } (1.15)\ \} \\
&join\, A \cdot join\, (\mathsf{List}\, A) \cdot \mathsf{List}\, (\mathsf{List}\, (guard\, p)) \\
=\ & \{\ \text{property of } join\ (1.23)\ \} \\
&join\, A \cdot \mathsf{List}\, (join\, A) \cdot \mathsf{List}\, (\mathsf{List}\, (guard\, p)) \\
=\ & \{\ \mathsf{List} \text{ is a functor } (1.11\mathrm{b})\ \} \\
&join\, A \cdot \mathsf{List}\, (join\, A \cdot \mathsf{List}\, (guard\, p)) \\
=\ & \{\ \text{definition of } filter\ (1.21)\ \} \\
&join\, A \cdot \mathsf{List}\, (filter\, p).
\end{aligned}
$$

Observe that the proof makes implicit use of Leibniz's context rules; see Section 1.2.

When writing or reading an equational proof, it is customary or even advisable to start at both ends, applying some obvious rewrites such as unfolding definitions. In the preceding example, we note that the loose ends can be connected by applying Property (1.23).

The previous calculation exemplifies an equational proof. The proof format works equally well for arbitrary *transitive* relations, for example $\leqslant$, $<$, or $\Longrightarrow$. The following calculation demonstrates that f is mono if $g \cdot f$ is mono:

$$f \cdot x_1 = f \cdot x_2$$
$$\Longrightarrow \quad \{ \text{ Leibniz (1.5c) } \}$$
$$g \cdot f \cdot x_1 = g \cdot f \cdot x_2$$
$$\Longrightarrow \quad \{ \text{ assumption: } g \cdot f \text{ mono (1.5a) } \}$$
$$x_1 = x_2.$$

1.7.2 Commutative Diagrams. Category theory has a strong visual flavor. Diagrams can be used to visualize not only arrows, but also properties of arrows, and to conduct proofs. We shall see that diagrammatic proof is an attractive alternative to symbolic proof.

Recall that a composite arrow can be visualized by a one-dimensional drawing of a path. To visualize an equality between two composite arrows, we can connect the corresponding paths at both ends, obtaining a two-dimensional drawing. As an example, the following equation on the left can be represented by the diagram on the right:

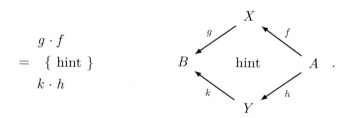

As noted before, the advantage of diagrammatic over symbolic notation is that it adds vital type information.

A diagram where all paths from the same source to the same target lead to the same result by composition is called a *commutative diagram*. A commutative diagram can represent an equation (see the definition of products and coproducts), but it can also serve as a proof. To illustrate, here is a proof of (1.22) framed as a commutative diagram. (For clarity, the unfolding of definitions is omitted and List is abbreviated to L.)

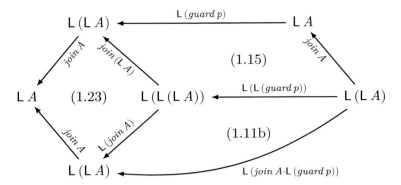

The outer pentagon represents the conclusion, the to-be-shown equation; the inner squares and triangles constitute the assumptions. One can show that, for the entire diagram to commute, it is sufficient that the inner diagrams commute.

Commutative diagrams work well for objects and arrows, but less so for categories, functors, and natural transformations. This is already evident in the previous example, where complex terms are used as labels, mixing symbolic and diagrammatic notation. We argue that string diagrams, developed in Chapter 2, are a better alternative.

Summary

A category consists of two components, objects and arrows. Functors are structure-preserving maps between categories, and natural transformations can be seen as mappings between functors. Categories, functors, and natural transformations form a so-called 2-category.

Categories generalize both monoids and preorders:

in **Cat**	in **Mon**	in **Pre**
category	monoid	preorder
functor	monoid homomorphism	monotone map
natural transformation	pointwise conjugation	pointwise preorder

There are many ways of constructing new categories from old: subcategories, opposite categories, product categories, and functor categories. Opposite categories are at the heart of the duality principle: categorical concepts come in pairs; duality cuts down the work by half. Product categories allow us to capture n-ary functors, and functor categories higher-order functors – functors that take functors as arguments or yield functors as results.

Further Reading

The basic concepts of category were introduced by Eilenberg and MacLane (1945), and this article is still very relevant.

The standard modern reference for basic category theory is the excellent Mac Lane (1998), although it does require a certain amount of mathematical experience to understand the examples. Stronger expository accounts are Awodey (2010), Leinster (2014), and the more computer science oriented Crole (1993). The recent Spivak (2014) is written specifically with practitioners outside mathematics in mind.

Modern encyclopedic accounts of large parts of category theory include Borceux (1994a,b,c) and Johnstone (2002a,b).

We use order theory and lattices in many of our examples. An enjoyable introduction to the fundamentals is Davey and Priestley (2002). Backhouse et al. (1998) provided an explicit development of category theory as a generalization of order theoretic notions.

Exercises

1.1 ○ Summarize the contents of this chapter in your own words.

1.2 ● Precisely define the categories mentioned in Section 1.1. What are the objects, what are the arrows? How are the identity arrows and composition of arrows defined?

1.3 ◉ Define a category whose objects are natural numbers and whose arrows of type $n \to m$ are real-valued matrices of dimension $m \times n$.

1.4 ◉ The category **Rel** features relations as arrows. Relations can also be part of the object data. Consider triples (A_1, R, A_2), where A_1 and A_2 are sets and $R \subseteq A_1 \times A_2$ is a binary relation. These triples form the objects of a category; an arrow between objects (A_1, R, A_2) and (B_1, S, B_2) is then a pair of functions (f_1, f_2) with $f_1 : A_1 \to B_1$ and $f_2 : A_2 \to B_2$ such that

$$\forall a_1 \in A_1 . \ \forall a_2 \in A_2 . \ (a_1, a_2) \in R \implies (f_1 \, a_1, f_2 \, a_2) \in S.$$

In words, the functions take related arguments to related results. Fill in the details by finding a suitable notion of composition, and identity arrows. Show that composition is both associative and unital. This category underlies Wadler's "Theorems for Free!" (Wadler, 1989).

1.5 ○ Are **Mon** and **Pre** subcategories of **Cat**? If yes, are they full?

1.6 ○ (a) Let $\mathcal{C}$ be a monoid category. What is the opposite category $\mathcal{C}^{op}$?
(b) Let $\mathcal{C}$ be a preorder category. What is the opposite category $\mathcal{C}^{op}$?

1.7 ⊙ (a) Let $\mathcal{C}$ and $\mathcal{D}$ be two monoid categories. What is the product category $\mathcal{C} \times \mathcal{D}$? (b) Let $\mathcal{C}$ and $\mathcal{D}$ be two preorder categories. What is the product category $\mathcal{C} \times \mathcal{D}$?

1.8 ⊙ Prove that g is split epi if and only if the partial application $g \cdot -$ is surjective (1.6c). Also show the dual statement (1.6d).

1.9 ○ Show that, if f has both a pre- and post-inverse, they must coincide.

1.10 ⊙ (a) Show that the isos in **Mon** are exactly the bijective monoid homomorphisms. (b) Show that the isos in **Pre** are *not* the same as bijective, monotone functions.

1.11 ● Prove the relations summarized in Figure 1.1 and show that the inclusions are proper: prove that a split mono is a mono and exhibit a mono that is not a split mono, and so on.

1.12 ● Explain why the notions of mono, epi, split mono, and split epi give rise to only seven different concepts (which ones?), even though there are $2^4 = 16$ different combinations of four properties.

1.13 ○ Find a category with multiple distinct initial and final objects.

1.14 ⊙ Show that the product of B_1 and B_2 is unique up to a *unique* isomorphism that makes the diagram

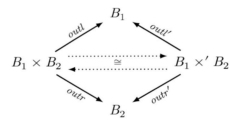

commute. (It is *not* the case that there is a unique isomorphism *per se*. For example, there are two isomorphisms between $B \times B$ and $B \times B$: the identity $id_{B \times B} = outl \,\triangle\, outr$ and $outr \,\triangle\, outl$.)

1.15 ⊙ Define the coproduct of two categories, dualizing the product of categories; see Definition (1.8). *Hint:* tag the objects and arrows; see Example 1.13. You must find a sensible way to define identity and composition.

1.16 ⊙ *Hint:* you need to solve Exercise 1.15 first. (a) Let $\mathcal{C}$ and $\mathcal{D}$ be two monoid categories. What is the coproduct category $\mathcal{C} + \mathcal{D}$? (b) Let $\mathcal{C}$ and $\mathcal{D}$ be two preorder categories. What is the coproduct category $\mathcal{C} + \mathcal{D}$?

1.17 ● Linear maps between two vector spaces form again a vector space. Does this imply that **Vect** $(\mathbb{K})$ has exponentials? *Hint:* you may want to peek at Exercise 4.7 first.

1.18 ◉ Does **Mon** have initial and final objects? What about coproducts and products (see also Exercises 1.7(a) and 1.16(a))? And exponentials (see also Exercise 1.25(a))?

1.19 ◉ Does **Pre** have initial and final objects? What about coproducts and products (see also Exercises 1.7(b) and 1.16(b))? And exponentials (see also Exercise 1.25(b))?

1.20 ⊙ Does **Rel** have initial and final objects? What about coproducts and products? And exponentials?

1.21 ⊙ This exercise aims to fill in some of the details of Example 1.21. Let A be a set, • a binary function on A, and e a fixed element in A. Define:

$$x \leqslant y \iff x \bullet y = y.$$

Show that:

- $\leqslant$ is reflexive if • is idempotent.
- $\leqslant$ is antisymmetric if • is commutative.
- $\leqslant$ is transitive if • is associative.
- If e is the unit element, then it is the least element of the order $\leqslant$.
- If $h : (A, \bullet, e) \to (B, \bullet, e)$ is a homomorphism of idempotent monoids, show that it is monotone with respect to $\leqslant$.

1.22 ⊙ Show diagrammatically that split monos and split epis are preserved by functor application. Conclude that functors preserve isomorphisms:

$$A \cong B \quad \Longrightarrow \quad \mathsf{F}\,A \cong \mathsf{F}\,B.$$

Are all monos and epis preserved by functors?

1.23 ◉ If we fix one argument of a bifunctor, we obtain a functor. The converse is not true: functoriality in each argument separately does not imply functoriality in both. Rather, we have the following: the map $- \otimes = \,: \mathcal{C} \times \mathcal{D} \to \mathcal{E}$ is a bifunctor if and only if the partial application $- \otimes B : \mathcal{C} \to \mathcal{E}$ is a functor for all $B : \mathcal{D}$, the partial application $A \otimes - : \mathcal{D} \to \mathcal{E}$ is a functor for all $A : \mathcal{C}$, and if furthermore the two collections of unary functors satisfy the *exchange condition*,

$$(f \otimes B'') \cdot (A' \otimes g) = (A'' \otimes g) \cdot (f \otimes B'), \tag{1.24}$$

for all $f : A' \to A'' : \mathcal{C}$ and $g : B' \to B'' : \mathcal{D}$. Given f and g there are two ways of turning $A' \otimes B'$ things into $A'' \otimes B''$ things. The exchange condition (1.24) demands that they are equal:

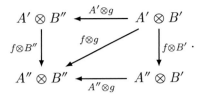

The arrow part of the bifunctor, the diagonal, is then given by either side of the equation. Prove the so-called exchange lemma.

1.24 ⊙ Fill in the details of Example 1.19. In particular, show that the arrow map of the bifunctor $- \times =$ satisfies the typing requirements and the functor laws. Dualize to coproducts. Show that $(-)^X$ is functorial.

1.25 ⊙ (a) Let $\mathcal{C}$ and $\mathcal{D}$ be two monoid categories. What is the functor category $\mathcal{D}^{\mathcal{C}}$? (b) Let $\mathcal{C}$ and $\mathcal{D}$ be two preorder categories. What is the functor category $\mathcal{D}^{\mathcal{C}}$?

1.26 ○ Continuing Exercise 1.24, show that *outl* and *outr* are natural transformations. Dualize to coproducts. Show that *apply* : $B^X \times X \to B$ is natural in B.

1.27 ⊙ How many natural transformations are there of type $\mathsf{Id} \overset{\cdot}{\to} \mathsf{Id}$, where $\mathsf{Id} : \mathbf{Set} \to \mathbf{Set}$? And of type $\mathsf{Id} \overset{\cdot}{\to} \mathsf{P}$, where $\mathsf{P}\, A = A \times A$? And if we flip source and target: $\mathsf{P} \overset{\cdot}{\to} \mathsf{Id}$?

1.28 ⊙ Continuing Exercise 1.23 show that functor application and functor composition are bifunctors:

$$\mathsf{Apply} : \mathcal{D}^{\mathcal{C}} \times \mathcal{C} \to \mathcal{D} \quad \text{and} \quad - \circ = \, : \mathcal{E}^{\mathcal{D}} \times \mathcal{D}^{\mathcal{C}} \to \mathcal{E}^{\mathcal{C}}.$$

1.29 ⊙ Does **Cat** have initial and final objects? What about coproducts and products? And exponentials?

1.30 ◉ Show that the following are equivalent for a category $\mathcal{C}$:

- For every category $\mathcal{B}$ and pair of functors $\mathsf{F}, \mathsf{G} : \mathcal{B} \to \mathcal{C}$, every transformation between F and G is natural.
- $\mathcal{C}$ is a preorder category.

1.31 ◉ Give an example of a functor that is fully faithful, but not injective on arrows. *Hint:* solve Exercise 1.15 first.

1.32 ⊙ Show the following implications:

$$\mathsf{F} \circ \mathsf{G} \text{ is essentially surjective} \implies \mathsf{F} \text{ is essentially surjective,}$$
$$\mathsf{F} \circ \mathsf{G} \text{ is faithful} \implies \mathsf{G} \text{ is faithful.}$$

1.33 ⊙ Show that $h : \mathsf{List}\, A \to \mathsf{List}\, B$ where

$$h \cdot join\, A = join\, B \cdot \mathsf{List}\, h$$

is a monoid homomorphism over the free monoid, assuming suitable properties of *join*. Conclude that *filter* is a homomorphism.

2

String Diagrams

We noted in Section 1.1 that there are two *one-dimensional* graphical representations of objects and arrows, one the Poincaré dual of the other. Likewise, there are two *two-dimensional* representations of categories, functors, and natural transformations.

The more traditional diagrammatic notation for these entities is known as a pasting scheme (Bénabou, 1967). These schemes represent categories by vertices, functors by (directed) edges between category vertices, and natural transformations as arrows in the region between functor edges, as illustrated here:

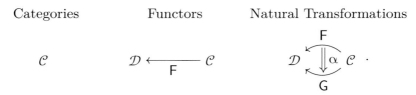

The dual graphical representations, called *string diagrams* (Street, 1996), are the focus of this monograph. Natural transformations are now vertices, functors are edges connecting natural-transformation vertices, and categories are regions between the functor edges or borders of the diagram:

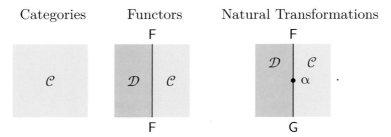

The edges are also called strings, hence the term "string diagram."

Again, we have two graphical representations to choose from. But which one to pick? We favor string diagrams, as they place the visual focus on the conceptually more significant natural transformations. There are practical considerations: vertices are easier to draw than regions; natural transformations are easier to string together (pun intended) if they are drawn as vertices rather than regions. A child would intuitively draw a string diagram by starting with the vertices, then "connecting the dots" with edges, and then finally "coloring in" the regions. In this way, we instinctively begin with the important natural transformations, and then fill in the secondary plumbing needed to connect them together in later steps.

But there is more to it than that. String diagrams provide category theory with a new and very distinctive visual flavor, supporting strong geometric intuitions. We hope to support this claim through a wealth of examples. Furthermore, we aim to demonstrate that string diagrams provide an effective tool for equational reasoning about elementary category theory.

In order to approach practical problems, it is important to be able to use *composition* to construct more complex structures and equations between them. We first consider composition of functors.

2.1 Composition of Functors

Given functors $G : \mathcal{D} \to \mathcal{E}$ and $F : \mathcal{C} \to \mathcal{D}$, in pictures,

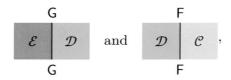

we saw in Section 1.4 that we can form their composite $G \circ F : \mathcal{C} \to \mathcal{E}$, drawn horizontally as follows:

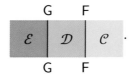

Notice how the graphical direction of composition follows the direction in the symbolic notation $G \circ F$. At this point, wires may only enter diagrams through the top border and exit through the bottom border, although we will slightly relax this restriction later. The source and target of the natural transformation described by a diagram may then be read from the top and bottom edges respectively. As a special case we represent the identity functor on a category $\mathcal{C}$, described in Section 1.4, by the corresponding region, without any associated edge:

$$\mathcal{C}$$

In this way, composing with identity functors "does nothing" in the diagrammatic notation, and so the equations between functors,

$$\mathsf{Id}_{\mathcal{D}} \circ \mathsf{F} = \mathsf{F} = \mathsf{F} \circ \mathsf{Id}_{\mathcal{C}} \qquad \text{or} \qquad \mathcal{D} \circ \mathsf{F} = \mathsf{F} = \mathsf{F} \circ \mathcal{C},$$

are handled silently by the notation. That said, occasionally it is helpful to draw an identity functor for emphasis; see for instance Example 3.8. We reserve a dashed line for this purpose.

Composition of functors is furthermore associative,

$$(\mathsf{H} \circ \mathsf{G}) \circ \mathsf{F} = \mathsf{H} \circ (\mathsf{G} \circ \mathsf{F}),$$

and again this property is built into the notation.

Recall that categories and functors between them form the category **Cat**. Comparing the preceding diagrams to the general diagrammatic notation for categories in Section 1, we observe that the original diagrams in a sense have been expanded to 2D for **Cat**: vertices have become vertical lines, and edges have become regions – imagine closing a blind. As we have seen in Section 1.4.2, the two-dimensional twist allows us to combine functors with objects and arrows:

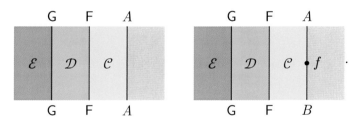

Objects and arrows *only* appear on the left boundary of a gray region. Normally the gray region will extend to the right boundary of the diagram, and the objects and arrows live in the region they border on their immediate left.

Remark 2.1. The gray region can be given a precise meaning using the terminal category **1**. Recall that **1** is the category with exactly one object and one arrow, the identity on that object. As usual, this category is displayed in string diagrams as a region:

We reserve this color for the category **1**, so that it can be easily identified. A functor of type $\mathbf{1} \to \mathcal{C}$ then picks out an object, and a corresponding identity arrow, in $\mathcal{C}$. In other words, we can identify an object $X : \mathcal{C}$ with a constant functor, $X : \mathbf{1} \to \mathcal{C}$. Now consider the special case of a natural transformation between two constant functors $X, Y : \mathbf{1} \to \mathcal{C}$. Such a natural transformation must have exactly one component, of type $X \to Y$. The naturality condition (1.15) becomes trivial, and so we can identify an arrow $f : X \to Y : \mathcal{C}$ with a natural transformation $f : X \overset{\cdot}{\to} Y : \mathbf{1} \to \mathcal{C}$:

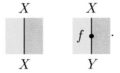

So, objects and arrows are special cases of functors and natural transformations, living on the left boundary of a gray region.   □

To reduce clutter, from this point on we will usually avoid labeling categories explicitly in diagrams. Specifically, we will omit category labels if they are clear from the surrounding context or if they are genuinely uninteresting. Where possible, we will consistently shade a category with the same color, even across multiple diagrams.

2.2 Composition of Natural Transformations

2.2.1 Vertical Composition of Natural Transformations. Given natural transformations,

we saw in Section 1.5 that we can form their vertical composite $\beta \cdot \alpha : F \overset{\cdot}{\to} H$. In string diagrams, we adopt the convention that vertical composition is ordered from top to bottom (hence the name "vertical") as in the following diagram:

Similarly to the notation for identity functors, the identity natural transformations of Section 1.5 are represented by the edge for the corresponding functor:

In this way, vertically composing with an identity natural transformation "does nothing" in the string notation, silently capturing the equations between natural transformations:

$$id_G \cdot \alpha = \alpha = \alpha \cdot id_F \qquad \text{or} \qquad G \cdot \alpha = \alpha = \alpha \cdot F.$$

Sometimes it is helpful to draw an identity natural transformation for emphasis; see, for instance, Example 3.8. We reserve an open circle for this purpose.

Vertical composition is, furthermore, associative,

$$(\gamma \cdot \beta) \cdot \alpha = \gamma \cdot (\beta \cdot \alpha),$$

and once more this property is built into the notation.

Recall that for fixed categories $\mathcal{C}$ and $\mathcal{D}$, functors of type $\mathcal{C} \to \mathcal{D}$ and natural transformations between them form the functor category $\mathcal{D}^{\mathcal{C}}$. For this category, the diagrammatic notation coincides with the general one introduced in Section 1.1, except that edges are now drawn vertically instead of horizontally.

Returning to the subject of integrating objects, note that the definition of vertical composition ensures that the following diagram,

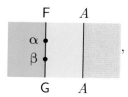

is unambiguous. The diagram can be divided into four parts; it does not matter whether we assemble the parts first horizontally and then vertically, or vice versa.

2.2.2 Horizontal Composition of Natural Transformations. There is a second form of composition for natural transformations. Consider natural transformations:

Generalizing the notion of composite for functors, we can form their *horizontal composite*, denoted $\beta \circ \alpha : H \circ F \dot\to K \circ G$, to be defined in the following discussion. Again the direction of composition in the string diagram parallels the symbolic notation:

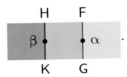

Turning to the definition of horizontal composition, we first single out two special cases where one of the arguments is an identity, which we write as a functor: $(H \circ \alpha)\, A := H\,(\alpha\, A)$ and $(\beta \circ F)\, A := \beta\,(F\, A)$. Readers may want to check that $H \circ \alpha$ and $\beta \circ F$ are indeed natural transformations. The horizontal composite $\beta \circ \alpha$ is then given by

$$(K \circ \alpha) \cdot (\beta \circ F) \;=:\; \beta \circ \alpha \;:=\; (\beta \circ G) \cdot (H \circ \alpha). \tag{2.1}$$

The two alternative definitions coincide by virtue of β's naturality. Some straightforward calculations show that horizontal composition is associative with $id_{\mathsf{Id}_{\mathcal{C}}} = \mathsf{Id}_{\mathcal{C}} = \mathcal{C}$ as its unit, justifying the graphical representation. Indeed, the definition of horizontal composition has an appealing visual interpretation. We obtain the vital *elevator equations* (Dubuc and Szyld, 2013), allowing us to move natural transformations up and down wires in an intuitive manner:

$$\tag{2.2}$$

The elevator equations generalize the naturality condition (1.16).

These two forms of composition are related by the important *interchange law*. The name indicates that the two transformations in the middle are interchanged:

$$(\delta \cdot \gamma) \circ (\beta \cdot \alpha) = (\delta \circ \beta) \cdot (\gamma \circ \alpha). \tag{2.3}$$

The law states that the relative nesting of horizontal and vertical composition does not matter. The diagram in the center of the following calculation therefore denotes a well-defined natural transformation:

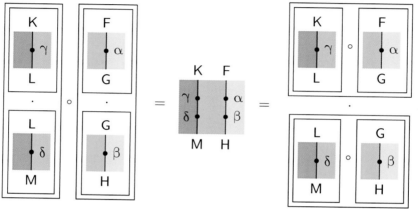

It does not matter whether we first combine the boxes vertically and then horizontally, or vice versa. Graphically, this law is subsumed by the notation.

Example 2.2. Continuing Example 1.28, we observe that the natural transformation *join* : List∘List $\dot{\to}$ List, which flattens a list of lists, can be defined using horizontal composition: *join* := U∘*reduce*∘Free. □

2.2.3 Natural Transformations between Composite Functors.
Finally we consider how to draw natural transformations between composite functors. For example, we could naively draw the natural transformation ψ : F∘G $\dot{\to}$ H∘J∘K∘L as:

This diagram is unsatisfactory, as it mixes symbolic and diagrammatic notation. Moreover, it does not make the structure of the input and output functors explicit, and it may restrict how we can compose and manipulate ψ in our diagrams. Alternatively, we can draw our diagram with each of the individual component functors connected as a separate input or output to ψ, resembling the arms and legs of, well, perhaps a small spider:

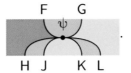

Observe that the arms and legs are drawn as bends, rather than as straight lines. In general, edges can be arbitrary curves with the important restriction that they *must not have a horizontal tangent (zero gradient)*. This way of drawing ψ is much more flexible, as it allows us to access the individual functors, F, G, H, J, K, and L, directly in our calculations.

2.2.4 Transformations. Spider-like diagrams also prove to be useful when dealing with plain transformations, for example, with transformations that we wish to establish as natural. Translated into string-diagrammatic notation, the naturality square (1.15) reads:

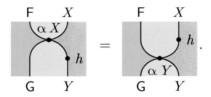

The diagrammatic rendering is instructive: naturality allows us to slide an arbitrary arrow up and down.

2.3 Converting between Symbols and Diagrams

In order for our graphical representations to be useful, we would like to be able to move back and forth between the traditional symbolic notation and string diagrams.

2.3.1 Symbols to Diagrams. We begin by converting a symbolic term into its corresponding graphical representation. Consider the expression

$$(\mathsf{H} \circ \mu) \cdot (\delta \circ \mathsf{S}) \cdot (\mathsf{T} \circ \delta),$$

where $\mathsf{H} : \mathcal{C} \to \mathcal{D}$, $\mathsf{S} : \mathcal{C} \to \mathcal{C}$, $\mathsf{T} : \mathcal{D} \to \mathcal{D}$, $\mu : \mathsf{S} \circ \mathsf{S} \xrightarrow{\cdot} \mathsf{S}$, and $\delta : \mathsf{T} \circ \mathsf{H} \xrightarrow{\cdot} \mathsf{H} \circ \mathsf{S}$. The significance of this expression will be discussed in ESD Chapter 3. For now, we solely concentrate on the mechanics of converting a symbolic expression to its graphical representation. We start by drawing the individual functors,

$$\mathsf{H} \;=\; \quad\quad \mathsf{S} \;=\; \quad\quad \mathsf{T} \;=\; \quad,$$

and natural transformations,

$$\mu \;=\; \quad\quad\quad \delta \;=\; \quad.$$

Observe that $\mathcal{C}$ is colored in yellow and $\mathcal{D}$ in orange. Next, we picture the three horizontal compositions by placing the components, in our case straight wires and spiders, next to each other. In general, we have to check that the corresponding regions match:

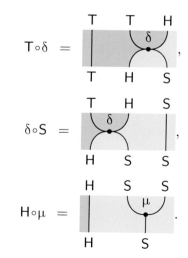

$$\mathsf{T}\circ\delta \;=\; \quad,$$

$$\delta\circ\mathsf{S} \;=\; \quad,$$

$$\mathsf{H}\circ\mu \;=\; \quad.$$

Finally, we stack the boxes vertically, connecting the output wires of each upper box to the input wires of its lower neighbor. In general, this involves checking that the number of wires and their types match. This is why we usually label at least the input wires (top border) and output wires (bottom border) of an entire box. As the final result we obtain

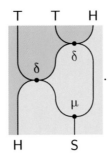

To recap, edges in string diagrams are implicitly directed, and we stipulate that the flow is from right to left for horizontal composition $\gamma \circ \alpha$, and from top to bottom for vertical composition $\alpha \cdot \beta$. Diagrams that differ only in the vertical position of natural transformations are identified – this is the import of naturality.

2.3.2 Exercising Artistic Licence. Notation matters greatly, both for understanding and for efficient calculation. Typesetters judiciously space formulas to guide the human eye. The typesetting program used for this monograph, TEX, makes very subtle distinctions to aid readability, for example, between binary operators and relations; the latter are surrounded by extra space. While these considerations are important in the one-dimensional case, they are almost vital in the two-dimensional case.

Drawing string diagrams is admittedly a bit of an art: good diagrammatic choices can make all the difference. Many, if not most, of the diagrams that appear in this monograph went through several iterations. First experiments with the two-dimensional notation invariably lead to very symmetrical drawings; early attempts of the authors were no exception to this rule. However, the full potential of string diagrams is unlocked only if the topological freedom inherent in the notation is exploited to aid the use of geometric intuition. We will see many examples of this throughout this book, beginning with the discussion of proofs in Section 2.4.1. To illustrate, consider the string diagram developed in the last section, repeated in the following diagram for convenience:

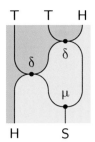 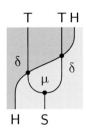 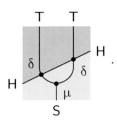

The curvy drawings of the incoming and outgoing edges lead to slightly amorphous regions, which is almost always an indication of bad design. It is actually preferable to draw some of the strings as straight lines crossed by a diagonal, exemplified by the diagram in the middle of the preceding illustration. If we additionally allow edges to enter and exit from the sides, then the layout can be further tidied up, obtaining the diagram on the right. Properties of natural transformations can often be interpreted as geometric "moves," for example, we shall encounter various properties where the diagonal line is moved across the natural transformation labeled μ. In a sense, the diagonal line is active, whereas the vertical lines are passive.

Of course, the redrawings beg the question of which movements are allowed. In general, string diagrams that are equivalent up to *planar isotopy* denote the same natural transformation. A planar isotopy is a continuous deformation of a plane diagram that preserves cusps, crossings, and the property of having no horizontal tangents. The proof by Joyal and Street (1991) depends on notions from topology and is outside the scope of this monograph. Returning to our examples, since we have only straightened edges, the transformations preserve the signs of the gradients. Consequently, all three diagrams denote the same composite natural transformation.

2.3.3 Diagrams to Symbols. In Section 2.3.1 we illustrated how to turn a symbolic expression into a string diagram. For the operation in the reverse direction, we use a *sweep-line algorithm*. Consider the following diagram, which involves four natural transformations:

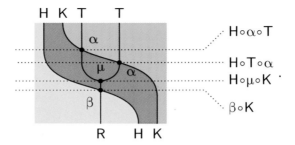

We shall discuss the significance of this composite at length in ESD Chapter 3. For now we consider how to systematically take it apart to recover an equivalent symbolic term. We sweep a horizontal line vertically from top to bottom, stopping whenever it meets one or more points. Then we write down, from left to right, the horizontal composition of all functors that cross the sweep line and all natural transformations that lie on the line. In our example, we thus obtain from top to bottom $H \circ \alpha \circ T$, $H \circ T \circ \alpha$, $H \circ \mu \circ K$, and $\beta \circ K$. The vertical composition of these terms then yields the desired symbolic representation. In our example this is

$$(\beta \circ K) \cdot (H \circ \mu \circ K) \cdot (H \circ T \circ \alpha) \cdot (H \circ \alpha \circ T).$$

As a by-product, we can conclude that natural transformations enjoy a "normal form": each natural transformation can be written as a vertical composition of horizontal compositions.

If we consider the case where we permit the freedom to have edges entering and exiting from the sides of diagrams, we must adjust for this first. To do this, we simply extend the diagram so that all edges exit from the top and bottom. For example,

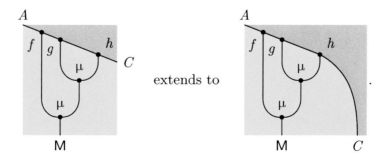

extends to

We can then scan down the diagram on the right to read off the horizontal composites:

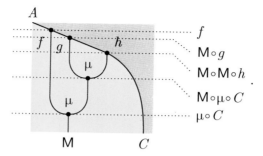

Note that we treat objects as constant functors, and arrows as natural transformations between them, see Remark 2.1. Finally, we compose these components vertically to recover a symbolic description of the entire diagram:

$$(\mu \circ C) \cdot (\mathsf{M} \circ \mu \circ C) \cdot (\mathsf{M} \circ \mathsf{M} \circ h) \cdot (\mathsf{M} \circ g) \cdot f.$$

As the entities on the far right of our diagram are ordinary objects and arrows, we can further rewrite their composite in more conventional notation as

$$\mu\, C \cdot \mathsf{M}\, (\mu\, C) \cdot \mathsf{M}\, (\mathsf{M}\, h) \cdot \mathsf{M}\, g \cdot f.$$

2.4 Equational Reasoning

Now that we have covered the basics of string diagrams, it is a good time to revisit the proof formats introduced in Section 1.7.

2.4.1 Diagrammatic Calculational Proofs. To see string diagrams in action, let us redo the proof of Property (1.22), systematically replacing symbolic by diagrammatic notation. To emphasize, we use string diagrams in defining equations, in to-be-established properties, and in calculational proofs. Starting with the former, the string-diagrammatic counterpart of *filter*'s definition (1.21), *filter* $p := join\ A \cdot \mathsf{List}\,(guard\ p)$, reads

$$ \tag{2.4} $$

The definition involves two arrows, *filter* p and *guard* p, and a natural transformation, *join*, correspondingly represented by three points. From the labels attached to the strings we learn that *filter p* is an arrow of type List $A \rightarrow$ List A. Applying the sweep-line algorithm gives Equation (1.21).

The subdiagram for *join* : List∘List $\xrightarrow{\cdot}$ List has two inputs and one output, resembling a tuning fork. It makes a second appearance in the counterpart of (1.22), *filter p* · *join A* = *join A* · List (*filter p*), the property that we wish to establish:

$$(2.5)$$

The proof of (2.5) hinges on a particular property of *join* (1.23), namely that the two ways of flattening a cubed list are equivalent: *join A* · List (*join A*) = *join A* · *join* (List A):

$$(2.6)$$

The string-diagrammatic rendering of (1.23) is arguably more perspicuous than the original symbolic version. If we view *join* as a binary operation – binary as it features two inputs – then the law essentially states that *join* is associative.[1]

Turning to the proof of (2.5), it suffices to unfold the definitions and to

---

[1] The List functor is an example of a monad, which includes *join* as part of its data. Equation (2.6) almost explains the slogan "a monad is *just* a monoid in the category of endofunctors," often used to intimidate Haskell newbies.

appeal to the associativity of *join*:

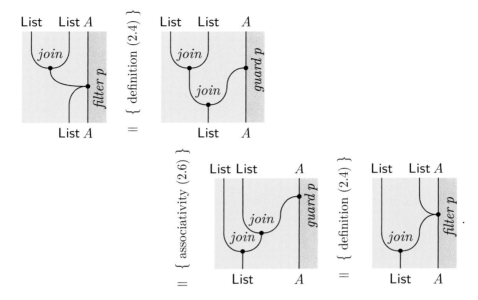

Quite pleasingly, there is only one nonadministrative step, the invocation of the associative law (2.6). Compared to the symbolic calculation in Section 1.7.1, there is no need to appeal to the functoriality of List or the naturality of *join*, as both laws are built into the diagrammatic notation. The proof clearly exhibits the central step; it also highlights that the arrow *guard p* plays no active role – the key step continues to hold if we replace *guard p* with any arrow of type $A \rightarrow$ List B.

We have essentially retained the proof format discussed in Section 1.7.1, except that we have replaced horizontal hints by vertical ones: this saves horizontal space to avoid stretching calculations over several pages.

2.4.2 Commutative Diagrams. Recall that a commutative diagram captures an equality between two composite arrows of the same type. It connects their one-dimensional representations as arrow-labeled edges between object-labeled vertices, at the corresponding end vertices, obtaining a two-dimensional object.

In principle, we can apply the same idea to string diagrams: to express an equality between two composite natural transformations, we connect their two-dimensional representations in the plane, obtaining a three-dimensional object. If you have difficulties visualizing the result, first imagine a two-dimensional commutative diagram whose edges are blinds; the desired three-dimensional object is obtained by opening the blinds. We said "in principle," as the idea does not really fly when working with a two-dimensional medium like a sheet of paper. Needless to say, three-dimensional drawings may also overextend our artistic skills.

In practice, commutative diagrams typically use a mixture of symbolic and diagrammatic notation, as already noted in Section 1.7.2. Recall that a natural transformation can be written as a vertical composition of horizontal compositions – the sweep-line algorithm outputs this "normal form." This suggests a disciplined approach, using diagrammatic notation for vertical composition and symbolic notation for horizontal composition. For illustration, Figure 2.1 displays a commutative diagram from Cheng (2011) that adheres to this discipline: edges are only labeled with horizontal compositions. We are not yet in a position to discuss the import of the proof – the material is only discussed in ESD Chapter 4 – so we only note that the diagram is rather impressive, consisting of 12 polygons of different shapes. However, nine out of 12 polygons are actually administrative ones, which appeal to naturality properties. By contrast, the corresponding proof using string diagrams consists of only two steps, carving out the essentials of the proof:

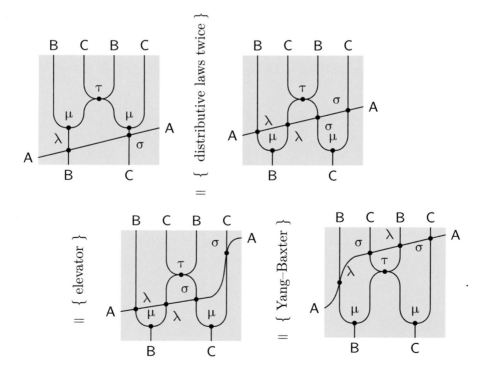

Visually, the proof proceeds by dragging a diagonal line (connecting the two

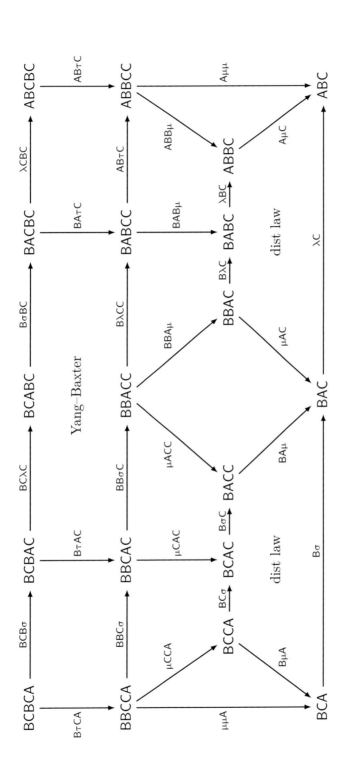

Figure 2.1 *Commutative diagrams in action (for reasons of space horizontal compositions are written by juxtaposition).*

occurrences of A) from bottom to top. Each time the line crosses a point, a property needs to be invoked. This happens exactly three times, hence there are three steps. (Well, almost – to avoid a horizontal tangent, we need to lift the rightmost point before the final drag.)

2.5 Natural Isomorphisms

A natural transformation is an arrow in a functor category. Thus, the qualifiers mono, epi and so on are also applicable to natural transformations. Of particular interest are natural isomorphisms – indeed, category theory was created to make this very notion precise. Recall: if the natural transformation $\alpha : F \to G$ has both a pre- and a post-inverse, then they coincide, and we denote them α°. In this case, α is a *natural isomorphism* with inverse α°, written $\alpha : F \cong G : \alpha^\circ$.

Diagrammatically, α and α° are natural transformations that annihilate each other if they touch in the right order:

If we have a natural isomorphism between composite functors, for example $\beta : F \to H \circ G$, then the graphical equations become

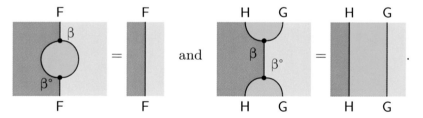

So, loosely speaking, inverses annihilate if *all* their arms and legs touch in the correct direction.

The definition of vertical composition implies that the components of a natural isomorphism are isos, as well. The converse is also true, but perhaps less obvious: if each αA is an iso, then α is a natural isomorphism with inverse $\alpha^\circ A = (\alpha A)^\circ$. Again, by definition of vertical composition, α° is both a post- and a pre-inverse of α. It remains to check that α° is natural. At first sight, it seems that we cannot use our graphical calculus, as it assumes naturality, whereas we aim to establish naturality. However, for the proof we need to argue about arrows, the components of the transformation, and these are straightforward to integrate into string diagrams. For example, that α and α° are componentwise inverses is captured by

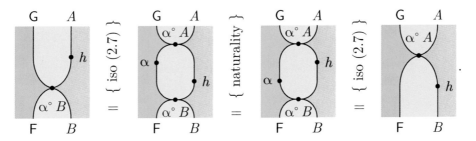

$$(2.7)$$

Observe the different graphical representations: the component of the *natural* transformation is given by two parallel lines with a dot on the left; by contrast, the component of the transformation is represented by a small spider with two arms and two legs, an "hourglass." (Of course, this is not the only option: Exercise 2.3 suggests a different drawing style.) Consequently, the to-be-established naturality condition is drawn as follows:

As the natural transformation α operates on the left and the arrow h on the right, we can appeal to the elevator equation to establish naturality:

We record:

$$\alpha \text{ iso} \iff \alpha A \text{ iso for all } A. \qquad (2.8)$$

As an aside, other properties are less well-behaved: a natural transformation that is componentwise split mono is not automatically convertible to a split mono natural transformation; see Exercise 2.2.

Most properties of functors are preserved under natural isomorphisms.

Let $F \cong G$, then

$$F \text{ essentially injective} \iff G \text{ essentially injective}, \tag{2.9a}$$
$$F \text{ essentially surjective} \iff G \text{ essentially surjective}, \tag{2.9b}$$
$$F \text{ essentially bijective} \iff G \text{ essentially bijective}, \tag{2.9c}$$
$$F \text{ faithful} \iff G \text{ faithful}, \tag{2.9d}$$
$$F \text{ full} \iff G \text{ full}, \tag{2.9e}$$
$$F \text{ fully faithful} \iff G \text{ fully faithful}. \tag{2.9f}$$

To train our calculational skills, let us establish these equivalences using string diagrams where appropriate.

For (2.9a) it suffices to show

$$F A \cong F B \iff G A \cong G B,$$

which holds as $F \cong G$ implies $F X \cong G X$ for all objects X, using furthermore that the relation $\cong$ is transitive. Likewise, for (2.9d) we show

$$F f = F g \iff G f = G g.$$

Let $\alpha : F \cong G$. We reason as follows:

Since α is an isomorphism, we can add it to and remove it from both sides of an equation. Starting in the middle, we can remove α by either post- or precomposing with α°, leaving either an F or a G wire behind.

Turning to surjectivity, for (2.9b) we need to show

$$(\forall B . \exists A . B \cong F A) \iff (\forall B . \exists A . B \cong G A),$$

which holds as $F X \cong G X$ for all objects X. Likewise, for (2.9e) we have to show

$$(\forall g . \exists f . g = F f) \iff (\forall g . \exists f . g = G f).$$

We show the left-to-right direction here. The other direction enjoys a symmetric proof:

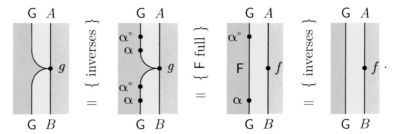

In the second step, we apply the assumption that F is full to the composite arrow $\alpha^\circ \cdot g \cdot \alpha : F A \to F B$, which gives us an f with $F f = \alpha^\circ \cdot g \cdot \alpha$.

2.6 Duality

We have briefly encountered duality in Chapter 1, but now that we have our graphical language in place, it is worth examining in more detail.

Opposite categories are key to precise discussion of duality within a category. Every notion in a category has a dual notion, given by interpreting the required axioms in the opposite category. For example, a category $\mathcal{C}$ has coproducts if $\mathcal{C}^{op}$ has products. As an aside, this approach of using the prefix "co" for dual concepts is applied somewhat inconsistently in category theory. The terms colimit, coproduct, comonad, and coalgebra are commonly used, but the terms final object and epi are preferred to coinitial object or comono.

We consider how $(-)^{op}$ acts on diagrams. Every category $\mathcal{C}$ yields a category $\mathcal{C}^{op}$, every functor $F : \mathcal{C} \to \mathcal{D}$ yields a functor $F^{op} : \mathcal{C}^{op} \to \mathcal{D}^{op}$, and every natural transformation $\alpha : F \dot\to G$ yields a natural transformation $\alpha^{op} : G^{op} \to F^{op}$. Notice the change of direction for the natural transformations. Recall that this change is formal, not actual, see Definition 1.7. So, $(-)^{op}$ flips diagrams vertically. For example, borrowing from the last section:

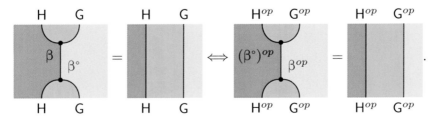

Here we use the same colors for categories and their duals. This is reasonable in this case as they can be disambiguated using the functor labels.

Flipping diagrams vertically in this way, we can introduce the *vertical dual* of any concept. Given the action of $(-)^{op}$ on diagrams, if some categories, functors, and natural transformations satisfy an equation, their opposites will satisfy the vertical dual condition.

But there is more to say: for every equation we can also flip our diagrams horizontally, yielding a *horizontal dual*. So, for example we may be interested in natural transformations,

satisfying the condition

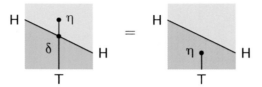

with respect to some natural transformations $\eta : \mathsf{Id} \xrightarrow{\cdot} \mathsf{S}$ and $\eta : \mathsf{Id} \xrightarrow{\cdot} \mathsf{T}$. (The overloading of the symbol η is intended to make the "move" being performed easy to follow.) Axioms such as these will be important for so-called Kleisli laws, which we will introduce in ESD Chapter 3.

It is generally worthwhile to consider the horizontal reflection of such a situation, in this case leading to a natural transformation:

satisfying the condition

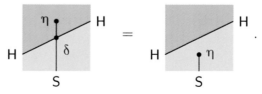

In fact, we will encounter a situation similar to this in ESD Chapter 3, in which both instances are equally important.

We will see various cases of both these forms of duality in later sections. Obviously, we can combine both horizontal and vertical duality to find yet another combination. So every structure involving functors and natural transformations is actually a member of a small family of mirror images.

Summary

String diagrams are the internal language of 2-categories. In the case of **Cat**, they represent natural transformations by vertices, functors are edges connecting natural-transformation vertices, and categories are regions between the functor edges or borders of the diagram. They are read like most *semitic* languages: from right to left and from top to bottom.

String diagrams are an effective tool for reasoning, as issues of associativity, functoriality, and naturality are handled silently by the graphical notation, allowing attention to be focused on the essential aspects of proof. String diagrams that are equivalent up to planar isotopy denote the same natural transformation. The topological freedom inherent in the notation can be exploited to aid the use of geometric intuition in the development of concepts and proofs.

Further Reading

String diagrams are a graphical formalism for working in category theory, providing a convenient tool for manipulating 2-cells within bicategories (Bénabou, 1967). For some background see Street (1995).

The first expository account of using string diagrams for elementary category theory we are aware of is Curien (2008b). Earlier developments of the ideas used in this monograph appear in Hinze and Marsden (2016a,b); Marsden (2015).

As monoidal categories are one-object bicategories, there is also a whole family of "monochrome" graphical calculi, carefully examined in the survey by Selinger (2011). Diagrammatic languages such as these have been used across many applications, for example, for entire textbook accounts of quantum theory (Coecke and Kissinger, 2017), semantics of natural language (Coecke et al., 2010), signal flow graphs (Bonchi et al., 2015), control theory (Baez and Erbele, 2015), Markov processes (Baez et al., 2016), analogue (Baez and Fong, 2015) and digital (Ghica and Jung, 2016) electronics and hardware architecture (Brown and Hutton, 1994), logic (Melliès, 2006), (Melliès, 2012), and even linear algebra (Sobocinski, 2019).

The technical foundations to make reasoning using string diagrams in monoidal categories rigorous are detailed in Joyal and Street (1998, 1991).

The mathematics of the connection to 2-categories and the setting for the colorful diagrams used in this book is described in Street (1996).

A calculational presentation of category theory was developed in Fokkinga (1992a,b) and Fokkinga and Meertens (1994). In these papers, we are presented with a choice of the traditional commuting diagram style of reasoning about category theory, and a calculational approach based on formal manipulation of the corresponding equations. We propose that string diagrams provide a third alternative strategy, naturally supporting calculational reasoning, but continuing to carry the important type information that is abandoned in the move to symbolic equations. Additionally, string diagram notation "does a lot of the work for free," an important aspect in choosing notation as advocated by Backhouse (1989).

Exercises

2.1 ⊙ Summarize the contents of this chapter in your own words.

2.2 ● Prove the following implications:

$$\alpha \text{ mono} \impliedby \alpha A \text{ mono for all } A,$$
$$\alpha \text{ epi} \impliedby \alpha A \text{ epi for all } A,$$
$$\alpha \text{ split mono} \implies \alpha A \text{ split mono for all } A,$$
$$\alpha \text{ split epi} \implies \alpha A \text{ split epi for all } A.$$

Show that the reverse implications do not hold in general. (This is the hard part.)

2.3 ⊙ Redo the proof of (2.8) exploring a different drawing style, where a component of a transformation is rendered as a horizontal blob:

2.4 ⊙ If $F : \mathcal{C} \to \mathcal{C}$ is an endofunctor, and $\alpha : \text{Id} \overset{\cdot}{\to} F$ an isomorphism, show that the following equation holds:

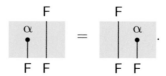

2.5 ◉ For a pair of functors F : $\mathcal{C} \to \mathcal{D}$ and G : $\mathcal{D} \to \mathcal{C}$ and natural isomorphisms α : G∘F $\xrightarrow{\sim}$ Id and β : F∘G $\xrightarrow{\sim}$ Id we can form two "hockey stick"-shaped diagrams as follows:

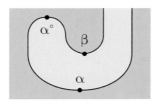 and 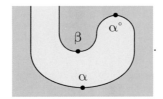 .

Prove that these two composites are equal.

2.6 ⊙ Assuming the following natural transformations,

$$\alpha : \text{Id} \xrightarrow{\sim} \text{Id}, \qquad\qquad \eta : \text{Id} \xrightarrow{\sim} \text{M},$$
$$\mu : \text{M}\circ\text{M} \xrightarrow{\sim} \text{M}, \qquad\qquad \rho : \text{Id} \xrightarrow{\sim} \text{M}\circ\text{N},$$
$$\sigma : \text{Id} \xrightarrow{\sim} \text{L}\circ\text{R}, \qquad\qquad \lambda : \text{H}\circ\text{T.} \to \text{M}\circ\text{H},$$

convert the following symbolic expressions into string diagrams:

(a) L∘α∘α∘R,

(b) L∘α∘R · L∘α∘R,

(c) μ∘N · η∘M∘N · ρ,

(d) μ∘N · M∘ρ · η,

(e) L∘M∘σ∘N∘R · L∘ρ∘R · σ,

(f) L∘(M∘σ∘N · ρ)∘R · σ,

(g) μ∘H · M∘λ · λ∘T.

Try to make the diagrams as colorful as possible.

2.7 ◉ Not all depictions of string diagrams convey the same visual intuition. The following proof is recreated from an academic paper (Street, 1995), mimicking the original linear style preferred by the author.

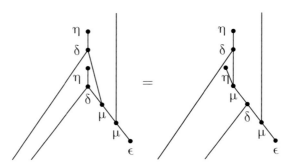

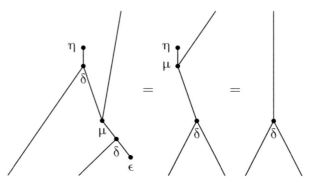

Try to adjust the design and layout in order to clarify what is going on. Do you recognize the equality shown?

2.8 ⊙ Use the sweep-line algorithm of Section 2.3.3 to convert the following diagram into symbolic notation:

Invent suitable names for the edges and points. Likewise, color and label the following diagrams (robots and almost-menorahs) and convert them into symbolic notation:

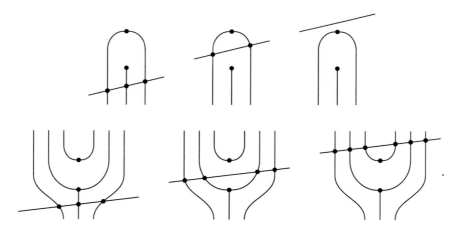

2.9 ⊙ Professor Bumstead has dumpling soup for lunch. As the dumplings are floating around,

he wonders whether the soup bowl could be captured by a string diagram. Can you help him? Do the dumplings' movements matter?

2.10 ◉ Invent categories, functors, and natural transformations so that the
happy snowman on the left in the following diagram becomes a valid
string diagram. You may need to add a few additional vertices to form
a legal diagram.

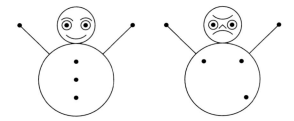

Someone has mischievously moved things around. Is the grumpy snowman the same as the happy snowman?

2.11 ⊙ Having studied the vertical sweep-line algorithm of Section 2.3.3,
Professor Bumstead wonders whether there is a horizontal counterpart?

2.12 ⊙ How many different types of string diagrams are there with at most
two inputs (arms) and at most two outputs (legs)? How many different
regions feature in each type of diagram? Try to find examples of each
type of diagram in the monograph.

2.13 ◉ How many different diagrams can you build using n "caps," where a
cap is a natural transformation of type $\mathsf{Id} \dashrightarrow \mathsf{F} \circ \mathsf{F}$ (no arms, two legs)?
For example, there are five diagrams using three caps.

These look like creatures peeking out from behind an invisible wall.

2.14 ◉ How many diagrams can you construct that contain each of the four
half-circles shown here exactly once?

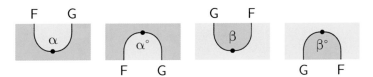

As usual, the edges and the regions have to match. There is, however,
no need to label edges and points, as they are uniquely identified by
the regions.

2.15 ⬤ (a) Given a single natural transformation of type $F \circ F \dot{\rightarrow} F$, a *fork*, how many diagrams are there of type $F^n \dot{\rightarrow} F$, where F^n denotes the n-fold composition of F with itself?

(b) Assuming the following identity, how many semantically different diagrams are there of type $F^n \dot{\rightarrow} F$?

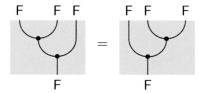

2.16 ⊙ Given a fork and its vertical reflection, a *cofork*,

how many different diagrams can you build of type (a) $F^1 \dot{\rightarrow} F^1$, (b) $F^1 \dot{\rightarrow} F^3$, (c) $F^3 \dot{\rightarrow} F^1$, or (d) $F^2 \dot{\rightarrow} F^2$? (Do not peek ahead. Exercise 2.19 solves this one, taking it further.)

2.17 ⬤ Assume that F, G, and H are endofunctors over some fixed category. Given natural transformations *red* : $G \circ F \dot{\rightarrow} F \circ G$, *orange* : $H \circ G \dot{\rightarrow} G \circ H$, and *blue* : $H \circ F \dot{\rightarrow} F \circ H$, we can "sort" the three functors (shown as wide blobs in the following diagram) in two different ways:

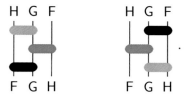

Sorting simply means that we construct a composite natural transformation of type $H \circ G \circ F \dot{\rightarrow} F \circ G \circ H$. (a) Draw string diagrams for "sorting"

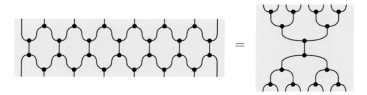

Figure 2.2 Nets and wristlets.

four endofunctors, using natural transformations for sorting two. How many building blocks are needed? (b) How many ways are there to sort four functors in total? (c) Assume that the two diagrams for sorting three functors are equal for all combinations of three out of four functors. Show that under these assumptions all diagrams for sorting four functors are equal. (d) Can you generalize the construction to n functors?

2.18 ◉ (a) Adapt the scheme of Exercise 2.17 to transform an arbitrary permutation of n functors into an ordered sequence. (b) How many building blocks are needed now? (c) Is the task any harder if arbitrary permutations are also permitted as outputs?

2.19 ◉ Given a fork and a cofork,

we can form one diagram of type $F^1 \dashrightarrow F^1$, two diagrams of both $F^1 \dashrightarrow F^3$ and $F^3 \dashrightarrow F^1$, and three diagrams of type $F^2 \dashrightarrow F^2$. If we identify the diagrams of the same type and equate the single $F^1 \dashrightarrow F^1$ diagram with the identity, we arrive at five axioms. Firstly, the equation known as the *special axiom*. The following are *associative* properties:

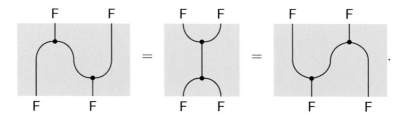

Finally, there are two *interaction axioms*:

(a) Prove the identity shown in Figure 2.2.
(b) Prove the so-called *spider theorem*: each connected diagram of type $F^m \dashrightarrow F^n$ is equivalent to a spider with m arms and n legs, an m-pronged fork placed on top of an m-pronged cofork. For example, the diagrams on the right-hand sides of Figure 2.2 are spiders. In other words, two connected diagrams are equal if they have the same type.

3

Monads

We now have enough machinery to explore more advanced categorical concepts using string diagrams. We start with mostly monochromatic diagrams in this chapter, which introduces monads, and then move on to more colorful pictures in Chapter 4, which deals with adjunctions.

3.1 Monads

Monads are one of the central concepts of category theory, arising naturally in many areas:

- To an algebraist, they capture algebraic theories in terms of their free algebras.
- To a topologist, they generalize the notion of closure operator.
- To a logician, they correspond to certain modalities in logic.
- To a computer scientist, monads model side effects such as state, exceptions, nondeterminism, probabilistic behavior, and input/output.
- To a Haskell programmer, they are a vital programming abstraction.

Historically, monads first appeared in the work of Godement (1964) with the uninspiring title *standard construction*. The equally dull term *triple* was introduced by Eilenberg and Moore (1965). The term monad seems to have been coined by Bénabou (1967), the name hinting at connections with monoids that we shall soon discuss. This term has now risen to dominance, probably due to its adoption in the standard text by Mac Lane (1998).

There are at least three different ways to introduce monads (Manes, 1976). For our purposes, the so-called monoid form, which is based on two natural transformations, is most useful. A *monad* consists of a functor $M : \mathcal{C} \to \mathcal{C}$

and natural transformations:

$$\eta : \mathsf{Id} \dot{\to} \mathsf{M},$$
$$\mu : \mathsf{M} \circ \mathsf{M} \dot{\to} \mathsf{M}.$$

Drawn as a string diagram, η looks a tad like a lollipop – recall that the identity functor is drawn as a region – whereas μ resembles a tuning fork:

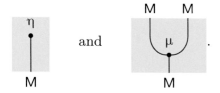

The diagrams are monochromatic as M is an endofunctor.

The natural transformations are required to satisfy the following *unit* and *associativity* axioms:

$$\mu \cdot (\eta \circ \mathsf{M}) = id = \mu \cdot (\mathsf{M} \circ \eta), \tag{3.1a}$$
$$\mu \cdot (\mu \circ \mathsf{M}) = \mu \cdot (\mathsf{M} \circ \mu). \tag{3.1b}$$

Written algebraically, these axioms are not particularly instructive. The equivalent string diagrams are much more revealing (ignore the trident for the moment):

$$\tag{3.2a}$$

$$\tag{3.2b}$$

Equations (3.2a) and (3.2b) make plain the idea that monads can be seen as monoids in an appropriate way, as hinted at by the suggestive names *unit* and *multiplication* given to η and μ. Since multiplication is associative, we will sometimes use a trident or three-pronged fork as a shorthand for two nested two-pronged forks.

Remark 3.1 (Monads from a Programming Language Perspective). Haskell programmers think of a monad as a mechanism that supports effectful computations (see also Section 3.4). A monadic program is an arrow of type $A \to M\,B$, where the monad is wrapped around the target. The two operations that come with a monad organize effects: η creates a pure computation, μ merges two layers of effects. The unit laws (3.1a) state that merging a pure with a potentially effectful computation gives the effectful computation. The associative law (3.1b) expresses that the two ways of merging three layers of effects are equivalent. ☐

A rather boring example of a monad is the *identity monad* Id with $\eta = id$ and $\mu = id$. Boring but useful.

Now that you have encountered the identity monad, you may hope to be able to compose monads, as well. However, even if endofunctors S and T carry monad structures, S∘T is *not* necessarily a monad. Do you see why? We might hope to form the following diagrams:

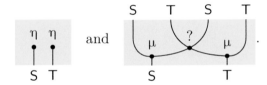

The diagram for the unit causes no difficulty. The problem is that the diagram for the composite multiplication is cheating. The wire crossing labeled with a question mark is the issue. *We are not allowed to cross wires in string diagrams*, so we cannot automatically form this picture. On the other hand, if we do not cross the wires, the S and T input wires will be in the wrong order. The only way to "cross" wires in our pictures and change their order is to introduce a natural transformation vertex of the appropriate type. We shall return to this idea in great detail later in ESD Chapters 3 and 4.

3.1.1 Examples of Monads. To make the abstract notion of a monad more accessible, we examine several examples, many of which will be important in later sections.

Example 3.2 (Preorders). A monad in a preorder category is a *closure operator*: a monotone map $c : \mathsf{P} \to \mathsf{P}$ that is extensive, $id \leqslant c$, and idempotent, $c \cdot c \cong c$. We write $id \leqslant c$ to denote the identity function being pointwise below the function that is constantly c. As c is extensive, the second condition can be weakened to $c \cdot c \leqslant c$. As an example, partially applied union $- \cup X$ is a closure operator. The reflexive, transitive closure of a relation is another example. ☐

Collection		Operations			Shorthand	Properties
		empty	singleton	join		AC I
trees	Tree	*empty*	*bud a*	*fork x y*	–	
lists	List	[]	[*a*]	*x y*	[$a_1, \dots, a_n$]	$\checkmark$
bags	Bag		*a*	*x* ⊎ *y*	$a_1, \dots, a_n$	$\checkmark\checkmark$
sets	Set	{}	{*a*}	*x* ∪ *y*	{$a_1, \dots, a_n$}	$\checkmark\checkmark$ $\checkmark$

Figure 3.1 The Boom hierarchy of collection types. (The last column in-dicates whether the binary operation is *A*ssociative, *C*ommutative, or *I*dempotent.)

Example 3.3 (Powerset). In Example 1.27 we noted that the maps *single* : Id $\dot{\to}$ Pow and $\bigcup$: Pow∘Pow $\dot{\to}$ Pow are both natural transformations. In fact, they provide the unit and multiplication for the *powerset monad* Pow : **Set** → **Set**. The instances of the monad laws,

$$\bigcup\{X\} = X = \bigcup\{\{x\} \mid x \in X\},$$
$$\bigcup(\bigcup\mathcal{X}s) = \bigcup\{\bigcup\mathcal{X} \mid \mathcal{X} \in \mathcal{X}s\},$$

probably have a familiar ring.   □

Example 3.4 (Collection Types). Various collection types form a monad: finite trees, finite lists, finite bags, and *finite* sets; see Figure 3.1. In each case, the unit forms a singleton collection and multiplication "flattens" a nested collection; for example:

$$\mu\mathbb{N}\{\{1,2\},\{\},\{4711\},\{2,3,5\}\} = \{1,2,4711,2,3,5\}.$$

Multiplication basically removes the inner brackets.   □

We consider two computationally motivated examples.

Example 3.5 (Exceptions and Maybe). If we introduce a set of excep-tions E, indicating different errors that can occur in a computation, there is a functor **Set** → **Set** sending a set to its disjoint union with E,

$$\text{Exc } A := A + E,$$

and natural transformations:

$$\eta\, A := inl \quad \text{and} \quad \mu\, A := id \, \triangledown \, inr,$$

marshaling data into the left component of the disjoint union, and identifying exception elements in different components. Together, these constitute the *exception monad* Exc. The special case when E is a singleton set models optional data values, and is referred to as the maybe monad: Maybe $A = A + 1$. □

Example 3.6 (State Monad). Many algorithms work by manipulating a global state. These algorithms cannot be captured directly in a pure functional programming language such as Haskell, as pure functions cannot modify state. This is where the *state monad* comes in. For a fixed set P of states, we define (on the left using "categorical combinators," on the right using programmatic notation – $\lambda x \,.\, e$ denotes an anonymous function):

$$\text{State } A := (A \times P)^P$$
$$\eta\, A := \Lambda\, (id\, (A \times P)) \qquad \eta\, A\, a := \lambda x \,.\, (a, x)$$
$$\mu\, A := (apply\, (A \times P))^P \qquad \mu\, A f := \lambda x \,.\, g\, y\, \textbf{where}\, (g, y) = f\, x.$$

We can then think of a function $f : A \to \text{State } B$ as a stateful computation. Given a start state x and input a, the call $f\, a\, x$ returns a pair consisting of the result of the computation, and the updated state. □

The next example nicely links monoids to monads.

Example 3.7 (Writer Monad). Every monoid $(M, e, \bullet)$ induces a monad, the "write to a monoid" monad or simply the *writer monad*. The functor underlying the monad is the product bifunctor partially applied to the carrier of the monoid:

$$M\text{-Wr} := (M \times -).$$

Perhaps unsurprisingly, the unit of the monoid is used to define the unit of the monad. Likewise, the multiplication of the monoid is used to define the multiplication of the monad:

$$\eta\, A\, a := (e, a),$$
$$\mu\, A\, (m, (n, a)) := (m \bullet n, a).$$

Popular applications of the writer monad include counting, $(\mathbb{N}, 0, +)$, and logging, $(\Sigma^*, [], +\!\!+)$. □

3.2 Monad Maps

Whenever a new class of mathematical structures is introduced, the definition of structure-preserving maps follows hard on its heels (Davey and

Priestley, 2002). Monads are no exception where these maps are variously called *monad morphisms*, *monad transformers*, *monad functors*, or, indeed, monad maps. We pick the last term, simply because it is the shortest.

Given a pair of monads over the *same* base category, $S, T : \mathcal{C} \to \mathcal{C}$, a *monad map* is a natural transformation $\tau : S \dashrightarrow T$ that preserves unit and multiplication:

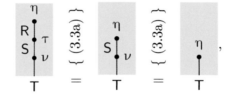

Again the string notation is instructive. Sliding the monad map up, it either disappears, or it "clones" into two branches. If we view the two monads as monoids, then τ is a monoid homomorphism, commuting appropriately with unit and multiplication.

The *identity* $id : T \dashrightarrow T$ is a monad map, and monad maps $\tau : R \dashrightarrow S$ and $\upsilon : S \dashrightarrow T$ compose. We simply apply the coherence conditions twice, sliding the monad maps up, one after the other:

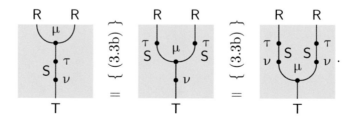

Composition is associative, and so monads on a category $\mathcal{C}$ and monad maps between them form a category, denoted $\mathbf{Mnd}(\mathcal{C})$.

Example 3.8. A perhaps incestuous example of a monad map is the unit

$\eta : \mathsf{Id} \dashrightarrow \mathsf{M}$, which sends the identity monad to M:

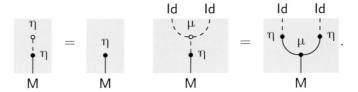

For clarity, we have added identity functors (dashed lines) and identity natural transformations (open circles) – recall that $\eta = id$ and $\mu = id$ for the identity monad Id. Because of (3.3a), the unit η is furthermore the unique monad map from Id to M (set $\mathsf{S} := \mathsf{Id}$, $\mathsf{T} := \mathsf{M}$). Categorically speaking, Id is the initial object in $\mathbf{Mnd}(\mathcal{C})$. $\qquad\square$

Example 3.9 (Emptiness). We have seen the monad $\mathsf{List} : \mathbf{Set} \to \mathbf{Set}$ in Example 3.4. We can think of $\mathsf{List}\, X$ as extending X with two new features: the ability to store multiple data values, and the ability to optionally store no data value at all. In fact, there are monads corresponding to these two features: the *nonempty list* monad List^+, and the monad Maybe of Example 3.5.

A similar analysis for bags and (finite) sets suggests the *nonempty bag*, *nonempty set*, and *nonempty powerset* monads, denoted Bag^+, Set^+, and Pow^+. In each case we have inclusion monad maps capturing the relationships between these monads:

$$\mathsf{Maybe} \dashrightarrow \mathsf{List} \dashleftarrow \mathsf{List}^+,$$
$$\mathsf{Maybe} \dashrightarrow \mathsf{Bag} \dashleftarrow \mathsf{Bag}^+,$$
$$\mathsf{Maybe} \dashrightarrow \mathsf{Set} \dashleftarrow \mathsf{Set}^+,$$
$$\mathsf{Maybe} \dashrightarrow \mathsf{Pow} \dashleftarrow \mathsf{Pow}^+.$$

We return to these inclusions in ESD Chapter 4. $\qquad\square$

Example 3.10 (Order and Multiplicity). A list is a collection of elements where order and multiplicity matters. Bags abstract away from order; the monad map *bagify* : $\mathsf{List} \dashrightarrow \mathsf{Bag}$ implements this abstraction step:

$$bagify\, A = reduce\,(\mathsf{Bag}\, A, , \uplus) \cdot \mathsf{Free}\; single,$$

where $single : A \to \mathsf{Bag}\, A$ maps an element, say, a to the singleton bag a. Sets further abstract away from multiplicity; there is a monad map *setify* : $\mathsf{Bag} \dashrightarrow \mathsf{Set}$. Their composition $setify \cdot bagify : \mathsf{List} \dashrightarrow \mathsf{Set}$ takes a list to a set, abstracting away both from order and multiplicity. $\qquad\square$

Example 3.11 (Writer Monad). We have seen in Example 3.7 that each monoid induces a monad, the so-called writer monad. Likewise, each monoid homomorphism induces a monad map between writer monads. Let

$$h : (M, e, \bullet) \to (N, e, \bullet)$$

be a monoid homomorphism; then the natural transformation

$$\tau : M\text{-Wr} \overset{\cdot}{\to} N\text{-Wr},$$

defined as

$$\tau\, A\,(m, a) := (h\, m, a),$$

is a monad map. As h preserves the unit, τ preserves the unit, as well:

$$\tau\,(\eta\, a) = \tau\,(e, a) = (h\, e, a) = (e, a) = \eta\, a.$$

As h preserves multiplication, τ preserves multiplication, as well:

$$\tau\,(\mu\,(m, (n, a))) = \tau\,(m \bullet n, a) = (h\,(m \bullet n), a) = (h\, m \bullet h\, n, a),$$
$$\mu\,(\tau\,(m, \tau\,(n, a))) = \mu\,(h\, m, (h\, n, a)) = (h\, m \bullet h\, n, a).$$

That the mapping works so seamlessly is, of course, not a coincidence. At a suitable level of abstraction, a monad *is* a monoid.[1] Pursuing this idea further is beyond the scope of this monograph.   □

3.3 Comonads

Monads dualize to comonads via vertical duality. A *comonad* consists of an endofunctor $N : \mathcal{C} \to \mathcal{C}$ and natural transformations:

$$\epsilon : N \overset{\cdot}{\to} \text{Id},$$
$$\delta : N \overset{\cdot}{\to} N \circ N.$$

Because of duality and because functors are drawn from top to bottom, the string diagrams for ϵ and δ are *vertical* reflections of the corresponding diagrams for η and μ:

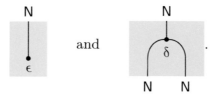

They have to satisfy dual axioms, the *counit* and *coassociativity* axioms, obtained by vertically reflecting the monad axioms:

[1] Perhaps you recall the slogan "a monad is *just* a monoid in the category of endofunctors."

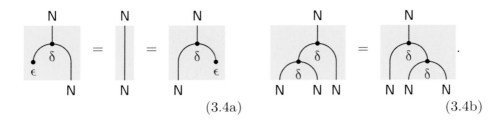

$$(3.4a) \qquad\qquad\qquad\qquad\qquad (3.4b)$$

As comonads arise via vertical duality, a comonad on $\mathcal{C}$ is "the same thing" as a monad on $\mathcal{C}^{op}$. As an aside, a structure that satisfies counit and coassociative laws is known as a *comonoid*. Although comonoids may be less familiar than monoids, they are a natural concept when viewed through categorical spectacles.

Remark 3.12 (Comonads from a Programming Language Perspective). One can think of a comonad as a mechanism that supports computations in context. A comonadic program is an arrow of type $N A \to B$, where the comonad is wrapped around the source. The operations that come with a comonad manipulate this context: ϵ discards the context, δ creates two copies of it. The counit laws express that doubling a context and then discarding one of the copies gives the original context. The coassociative law requires that the two ways of creating three copies of a context are equivalent. □

Example 3.13 (Preorders). A comonad in a preorder category is a *kernel operator*: a monotone map $c : P \to P$ that is reductive, $c \leqslant id$, and idempotent, $c \cong c \cdot c$. As c is reductive, the second condition can be weakened to $c \leqslant c \cdot c$. As an example, partially applied intersection $- \cap X$ is a kernel operator. The floor function $\lfloor - \rfloor : \mathbb{R} \to \mathbb{R}$, which assigns to every real x the greatest integer less than or equal to x, is another example. □

Example 3.14 (Nonempty List Comonad). We saw in Example 3.9 that nonempty lists form a monad. They also form a *comonad*, with counit $\epsilon :$ $\mathsf{List}^+ \dashrightarrow \mathsf{Id}$ extracting the last element of the list, and comultiplication $\delta :$ $\mathsf{List}^+ \dashrightarrow \mathsf{List}^+ \circ \mathsf{List}^+$ sending a nonempty list to the nonempty list of all its nonempty prefixes; for example:

$$\epsilon\, X\, [x, y, z] = z \qquad \text{and} \qquad \delta\, X\, [x, y, z] = [[x], [x, y], [x, y, z]].$$

Writing the list of prefixes in a two-dimensional way as on the left as follows,

    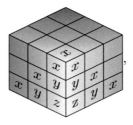

the counital laws state that the last column and the last row give the original list. The coassociative law captures that the two ways of forming a three-dimensional cube are equivalent. □

Example 3.15 (Costate Comonad). In Example 3.6 we built a state monad, exploiting Cartesian products, exponentials, and currying. By "reversing the order" there is a dual construction yielding the *costate comonad* CoState : **Set** → **Set**, for a fixed set of positions P:

$$\text{CoState } A := A^P \times P$$

$$\epsilon A := apply\ A \qquad\qquad \epsilon A\ (f, x) := f\ x$$
$$\delta A := (\Lambda\ id\ (A^P \times P)) \times P \qquad \delta A\ (f, x) := (\lambda y\ .\ (f, y), x).$$

We can think of elements of A^P as a table of A-values, one for each position in P. A map $A^P \to B^P$ transforms a table of A-values into a table of B-values. Uncurrying, these correspond to functions $A^P \times P \to B$, which calculate the value of a particular position in the table of B-values on request. The counit ϵ corresponds to doing nothing to the original table, by simply extracting values from the original table based on their original position.

Now consider the situation where we have maps $f :$ CoState $A \to B$ and $g :$ CoState $B \to C$. If we are given a table of A-values, using f and g, how can we calculate an element of a table of C-values? Clearly, we want to use g, but this requires a complete table of B-values. We can produce such a table by running f multiple times, once for each position. The action of the counit δ sets up this calculation by providing a table of inputs for f at each position, paired with a record of which position we need to produce in the final output by applying g. □

3.4 Kleisli Categories

Part of the beauty of monad theory is captured in two canonical categories associated with every monad. In this section we explore the Kleisli category of a monad (Kleisli, 1965). In the following section we move on to the Eilenberg–Moore category (Eilenberg and Moore, 1965). Both serve nicely as examples of manipulating "ordinary" arrows using string diagrams.

For a monad (M, η, μ), the *Kleisli category*, denoted $\mathcal{C}_\mathsf{M}$, has the same objects as $\mathcal{C}$ but the arrows differ. A Kleisli arrow $A \to B : \mathcal{C}_\mathsf{M}$ is an arrow of type $A \to \mathsf{M}\, B : \mathcal{C}$ in the underlying category.

Before we turn to the definition of Kleisli identity and composition, let us first explore some possible ways of drawing Kleisli arrows. A few options are:

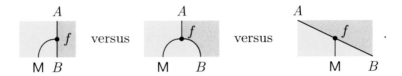

First experiments with the two-dimensional notation invariably led to very symmetrical drawings, like the diagram in the middle. After some iterations we discarded drawings based on this style in favor of the diagram type on the left, as it allowed us to line up several monadic arrows on the straight vertical edge. The final drawings seen in the following discussion, however, replace the vertical edge by a "minor" diagonal instead; see the diagram on the right of the preceding graphic. This enables us to draw the outgoing M edge as a straight vertical, which blends well with the way we have drawn the monad operations. To appreciate the choice, you may want to redo the following definitions and calculations in the other two styles.

When drawing diagonals, it is often convenient to allow edges to enter or exit the sides of diagrams; see Section 2.3.2. Recall: as edges must not have zero gradient, they can be extended unambiguously to a diagram in which all edges enter from the top and exit from the bottom of the diagram. For example:

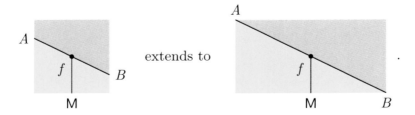

Turning to the definition of the Kleisli category $\mathcal{C}_\mathsf{M}$, the identity on A is given by $\eta\, A : A \to \mathsf{M}\, A : \mathcal{C}$, graphically,

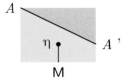

and the *Kleisli composite* of the two arrows $f : A \to \mathsf{M}\, B : \mathcal{C}$ and $g : B \to \mathsf{M}\, C : \mathcal{C}$, denoted $(f\,;g) : A \to \mathsf{M}\, C : \mathcal{C}$, is given by, combining symbolic and diagrammatic notation as follows:

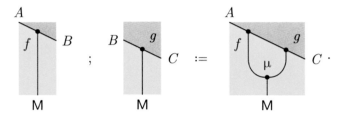

Observe that we use forward composition $f\,;g$ ("first f, then g") for Kleisli arrows, as this blends well with the graphical notation.

That our proposed identity arrows act as units with respect to composition, symbolically $id_A\,;f = f$ and $f\,;id_B = f$, can be seen from the following equalities exploiting the monad unit axiom (3.2a). For identity on the left:

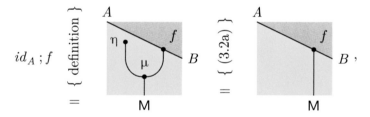

and for identity on the right:

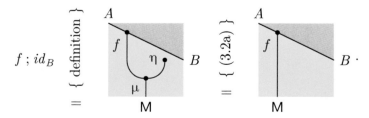

Notice how we seamlessly combine arrows and natural transformations in our diagrams. The string diagram notation also means we do not need to reason explicitly using the components $\eta\, A$ and $\eta\, B$, instead using η directly, making it easier to identify the applicable axioms. Associativity of composition, symbolically $(f\,;\,g)\,;\,h = f\,;\,(g\,;\,h)$, is proved similarly, following as a direct consequence of the associativity axiom (3.2b):

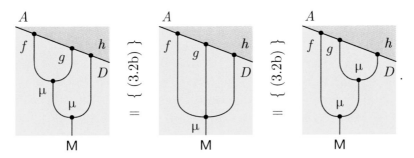

Again, we can manipulate μ directly, with the arrows f, g, and h playing only a passive role.

Remark 3.16 (Stateful Computations). When introducing the state monad in Example 3.6, we saw that arrows of type $A \to \mathsf{State}\,B$ could be thought of as stateful computations. The Kleisli category makes this observation significantly more useful, as we can now compose stateful computations. The unit η serves as the identity, a function that returns its input without modifying the state. The multiplication μ does exactly the right job of threading state from one computation to the next in the composition of the Kleisli category. □

Example 3.17 (Identity). We have noted that the identity functor $\mathsf{Id} : \mathcal{C} \to \mathcal{C}$ is a monad. Its Kleisli category $\mathcal{C}_{\mathsf{Id}}$ is morally the same as the category $\mathcal{C}$. We actually identify the two categories – occasionally, it is useful to view a category as a trivial Kleisli category. □

Example 3.18 (Maybe). A function $f : X \to Y + 1$ can be thought of as a partial function; we consider $f\,x$ landing in the right component to denote being undefined. With this observation in mind, the Kleisli category $\mathsf{Set}_{\mathsf{Maybe}}$ is isomorphic to the category of sets and partial functions. □

Example 3.19 (Powerset). Given a relation $R \subseteq X \times Y$ between sets X and Y, we can construct a function $r : X \to \mathcal{P}\,Y$:

$$r\,x := \{\, y \mid x\,R\,y \,\}.$$

In the other direction, given a function $r : X \to \mathcal{P}\,Y$, we can construct a relation $R \subseteq X \times Y$:

$$x\,R\,y \quad :\Longleftrightarrow \quad r\,x \ni y.$$

These constructions form a bijection. In fact, the Kleisli category $\mathbf{Set}_{\mathsf{Pow}}$ is isomorphic to the category $\mathbf{Rel}$ of sets and relations.   □

3.5 Eilenberg–Moore Categories

The Kleisli category is important to computer scientists, capturing various notions of computational effects such as state or nondeterminism. On the other hand, the Eilenberg–Moore category is of great mathematical interest, intimately connected to universal algebra. From the perspective of the Eilenberg–Moore construction, monads are algebraic theories, and their algebras are models of these theories.

To introduce Eilenberg–Moore categories, we proceed in two stages. Firstly, we introduce algebras for an endofunctor. These are unrestricted structures and can be thought of as implementing some signature of operations. We then move on to consider how to encode structures satisfying equational laws; for example, commutativity, associativity, or idempotence as commonly crop up in various forms of algebra such as group theory or linear algebra.

3.5.1 Algebras and Homomorphisms. As a further example of manipulating "ordinary" arrows using string diagrams, we consider algebras and their homomorphisms. Given an endofunctor $\mathsf{F} : \mathcal{C} \to \mathcal{C}$, an F-*algebra* is a pair (A, a), where A is an object in $\mathcal{C}$, and $a : \mathsf{F}\,A \to A$ is an arrow in $\mathcal{C}$, which are known as the *carrier* and *action* of the algebra. An F-*homomorphism* between algebras (A, a) and (B, b) is an arrow $h : A \to B$ in the underlying category $\mathcal{C}$ such that the *homomorphism axiom* holds:

$$h \cdot a = b \cdot \mathsf{F}\,h. \tag{3.5}$$

Turning to the string-diagram representation, the carrier of an algebra can be seen as static, which is why it is drawn as a "minor" diagonal:

Observe that the diagram is a vertical reflection of the diagram for a Kleisli arrow (except for the types). This is not a coincidence, as we shall see later.

The homomorphism condition (3.5) has an appealing visual interpretation:

$$\vcenter{\hbox{\includegraphics{}}} \quad = \quad \vcenter{\hbox{\includegraphics{}}} . \tag{3.6}$$

It allows us to slide h along the wire across the action a, which is trans-mogrified into b in the process. The property of *filter* (1.22) that we have shown both symbolically and diagrammatically is an instance of the homo-morphism condition.

To see that the identity $id : A \to A$ is an F-algebra homomorphism, we have to show $a \cdot \mathsf{F}\, id = id \cdot a$. In string diagrams this reduces to the following tautology:

$$\vcenter{\hbox{}} \quad = \quad \vcenter{\hbox{}} .$$

As composition is performed in the underlying category, it follows immedi-ately that $id \cdot h = h$, $h \cdot id = h$, and $(j \cdot h) \cdot k = j \cdot (h \cdot k)$. If we consider a pair of homomorphisms $h : (A, a) \to (B, b)$ and $k : (B, b) \to (C, c)$, we see that F-homomorphisms compose, as follows:

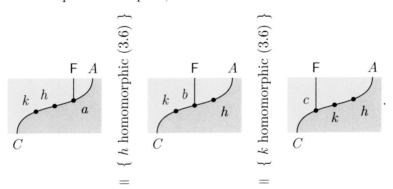

We first slide h across a, turning it into b, and then slide k across b, turning it into c. Since F-homomorphisms compose and have an identity, it follows that F-algebras and F-homomorphisms form a category, which is denoted F-**Alg**($\mathcal{C}$).

Example 3.20 (Preorders). Recall that a functor on a preorder category $\mathcal{C}$ is a monotone function $h : \mathcal{C} \to \mathcal{C}$. An h-algebra is an element $c \in \mathcal{C}$ such that $h\, c \leqslant c$. These are often referred to as *prefix points* of h. The arrows in h-$\mathbf{Alg}(\mathcal{C})$ describe the order between these prefix points. For example, the Kleene star a^* is the least prefix point of $h\,x = 1 + a \cdot x$.   □

Example 3.21 (Monoids). An endofunctor on a monoid category M is simply a monoid homomorphism $F : M \to M$. Algebras for F are arbitrary elements of M. For algebras $a, b \in M$, an arrow $h : a \to b$ is an element $h \in M$ such that $b \circ F\,h = h \circ a$.   □

Example 3.22 (Signatures, Monoids, and Binary Trees). Consider the *signature* or *interface* consisting of a constant and a binary operation:

$$leaf : A,$$
$$fork : A \times A \to A.$$

Observe that both operations share the same target type, which allows us to express the signature using a polynomial functor $\Sigma : \mathbf{Set} \to \mathbf{Set}$.

$$A \times (A \times A \to A) \cong (1 \to A) \times (A \times A \to A) \cong (1 + A \times A) \to A$$

The chain of isomorphisms suggests defining $\Sigma\,A = 1 + A \times A$.

The category Σ-$\mathbf{Alg}(\mathbf{Set})$ contains as objects implementations of the interface. For example, a monoid $(A, e, \bullet)$ can be turned into a Σ-algebra (A, a) setting $a\,(inl\,()) := e$ and $a\,(inr\,(x, y)) := x \bullet y$. As to be expected, Σ-homomorphisms between these Σ-algebras are exactly the monoid homomorphism. However, since we did not impose any restrictions on the signature, the category Σ-$\mathbf{Alg}(\mathbf{Set})$ also contains algebras which aren't monoids. An important example is afforded by the *initial* Σ-algebra, which can be thought of as the type of binary trees:

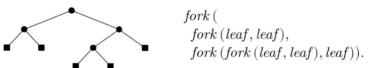

$$fork\,($$
$$\quad fork\,(leaf, leaf),$$
$$\quad fork\,(fork\,(leaf, leaf), leaf)).$$

In a sense, the operations of the signature are interpreted by themselves; the operations are turned into data constructors.   □

Example 3.23 (Identity). Examples involving identities are typically trivial. The category Id-$\mathbf{Alg}(\mathcal{C})$ of Id-algebras and Id-homomorphisms is an exception to this rule. Its objects are endofunctions and its arrows are commutative squares:

$$
\begin{array}{ccc}
\begin{array}{ccc}
C & \xleftarrow{k} & B \\
{\scriptstyle c}\downarrow & & \downarrow{\scriptstyle b} \\
C & \xleftarrow{k} & B
\end{array}
\;\cdot\;
\begin{array}{ccc}
B & \xleftarrow{h} & A \\
{\scriptstyle b}\downarrow & & \downarrow{\scriptstyle a} \\
B & \xleftarrow{h} & A
\end{array}
&=&
\begin{array}{ccccc}
C & \xleftarrow{k} & B & \xleftarrow{h} & A \\
{\scriptstyle c}\downarrow & & \downarrow{\scriptstyle b} & & \downarrow{\scriptstyle a} \\
C & \xleftarrow{k} & B & \xleftarrow{h} & A
\end{array}
\;\cdot
\end{array}
$$

The category Id-**Alg**($\mathcal{C}$) is nontrivial because the signature captured by Id is nontrivial: it consists of a single unary endofunction.   □

3.5.2 Algebras for a Monad. Next we consider algebras for a monad. Given a monad M : $\mathcal{C} \to \mathcal{C}$, an *algebra for* M, also referred to as an *Eilenberg–Moore algebra for* M, is an M-algebra (A, a) that satisfies the *unit* and *multiplication* axioms, or coherence conditions:

$$a \cdot \eta\, A = id, \tag{3.7a}$$
$$a \cdot \mu\, A = a \cdot \mathsf{M}\, a. \tag{3.7b}$$

Again it is instructive to turn the algebraic formulation into string diagrams.

$$\tag{3.8a}$$

$$\tag{3.8b}$$

Unit and multiplication of the monad are "absorbed" by the diagonal, leaving zero or two instances of the action a behind.

The category of M-algebras and their homomorphisms is known as the *Eilenberg–Moore category* of M, denoted $\mathcal{C}^{\mathsf{M}}$.

Example 3.24 (Identity). We have seen in Example 3.23 that the category of Id-algebras has an interesting structure. By contrast, the Eilenberg–Moore category $\mathcal{C}^{\mathsf{Id}}$ adds nothing to $\mathcal{C}$ – it is morally the same as $\mathcal{C}$. To see why, consider the algebra (A, a) for the monad Id. The coherence conditions specialize to $a = id$ and $a = a \cdot a$. So the action is necessarily the identity. We identify the two categories – occasionally, it is useful to view a category as a trivial Eilenberg–Moore category.   □

We noted at the beginning of the chapter that, to an algebraist, monads capture algebraic theories in terms of their free algebras. The following example illustrates this perspective, exhibiting a one-to-one correspondence between collection types and corresponding algebraic theories.

Example 3.25 (Collection Types and Algebras). Given an algebra for the list monad, (A, a) with $a :$ List $A \to A$, we can construct a monoid $(A, e, \bullet)$ with unit and multiplication:

$$e := a\,[\,], \tag{3.9a}$$
$$x \bullet y := a\,[x, y]. \tag{3.9b}$$

In some sense, e can be seen as a nullary version of a and $\bullet$ as a binary version. Conversely, a can be seen as an n-argument version of the two monoid ingredients. For the list monad, we can specialize the Eilenberg–Moore algebra unit (3.7a) and multiplication (3.7b) axioms to obtain

$$a\,[x] = x, \tag{3.9c}$$
$$a\,[a\ xs, a\ ys] = a\,(xs + ys). \tag{3.9d}$$

Using these equations, we confirm our monoid satisfies the monoid unit and associativity axioms:

$e \bullet x$
$=$ { definition of e (3.9a) }
$a\,[a\,[\,], x]$
$=$ { (3.9c) }
$a\,[a\,[\,], a\,[x]]$
$=$ { (3.9d) }
$a\,[x]$
$=$ { (3.9c) }
x.

$x \bullet (y \bullet z)$
$=$ { definition of $\bullet$ (3.9b) }
$a\,[x, a\,[y, z]]$
$=$ { (3.9c) }
$a\,[a\,[x], a\,[y, z]]$
$=$ { (3.9d) }
$a\,[x, y, z]$

The proof of the right unit axiom is similar. For associativity, we can also transform $(x \bullet y) \bullet z$ to $a\,[x, y, z]$ completing the proof.

Conversely, given a monoid $(A, e, \bullet)$, we can define an Eilenberg–Moore algebra on A as follows:

$$a = reduce\,(A, e, \bullet).$$

It is straightforward to confirm the Eilenberg–Moore algebra axioms.

If we consider homomorphisms, a function $h : A \to B$ is a list monad homomorphism $h : (A, a) \to (B, b)$ if and only if

$$h\,(a\,[x_1, \ldots, x_n]) = b\,[h\,x_1, \ldots, h\,x_n].$$

Properties	Monad	Description	Algebra
e i •			
$\checkmark$ – –	Maybe	optional values	pointed sets
– – $\checkmark$	Tree	binary trees	magma
– – A	List$^+$	finite, nonempty lists	semigroup
– – AC	Bag$^+$	finite, nonempty bags	commutative semigroup
– – ACI	Set$^+$	finite, nonempty sets	semilattice
– – ACI	Pow$^+$	nonempty sets	complete$^+$ semilattice ^{a}
U – A	List	finite lists	monoid
U – AC	Bag	finite bags	commutative monoid
U – ACI	Set	finite sets	bounded semilattice
– – ACI	Pow	sets	complete semilattice
U N A	Group	free group	group
U N AC	Ab	free commutative group	commutative group

Figure 3.2 Collection types and their algebraic theories. (The first column indicates whether a constant e, unary function i, and binary operation • are present. Beyond **U**nitality axioms, we also state which other axioms apply, from **A**ssociativity, **C**ommutativity, **I**dempotence, and i**N**verse.)

^{a} A lattice with joins of all nonempty sets

This is equivalent to the homomorphism condition between the corresponding monoids:

$$h\,e = e \qquad \text{and} \qquad h\,(x \bullet y) = h\,x \bullet h\,y.$$

The analysis shows that $\mathbf{Set}^{\text{List}}$ is isomorphic to the category of monoids and monoid homomorphisms. The point here is that, due to unitality and associativity, all that matters in a term in the theory of monoids is the list of variables that appear.

We can perform similar analyses to show that monads for various collection types correspond to various algebraic theories. For example, $\mathbf{Set}^{\text{Bag}}$ is equivalent to the category of commutative monoids, and $\mathbf{Set}^{\text{Set}}$ is equivalent to the category of bounded join-semilattices. Many other collection types arise in this way; see Figure 3.2. $\qquad\qquad\square$

Example 3.26 (Writer Monad). In Example (1.5) we have introduced the category of actions. Eilenberg–Moore's construction links this category to the writer monad discussed in Example 3.7. The Eilenberg–Moore category of the writer monad *is* the category of actions. The coherence conditions, (1.2a) and (1.2b), capture that unit and multiplication, (3.7a) and (3.7b), are respected; the defining property of equivariant functions (1.3) is the homomorphism axiom (3.5).

Example 1.29 also looked at the category of actions, but from a different angle: we observed that the category of actions is isomorphic to a functor category, indicating a close connection between the homomorphism axiom and the naturality condition.   □

3.6 Actions of a Monad

3.6.1 Left Actions. We have previously encountered monoid actions on a set. We now generalize that idea to monad actions on a functor. This lays the ground for material in Section 5.3.4, and hints at the notion of distributive law, to feature prominently in ESD.

Given a monad (M, η, μ) on a category $\mathcal{C}$, a *left action of* M on a functor $A : \mathcal{B} \to \mathcal{C}$ is a natural transformation $\alpha : M \circ A \xdot\to A$,

,

that respects unit and multiplication:

$$\eta \quad \alpha \; = \; \Big| \qquad (3.10a) \qquad \mu \; \alpha \; = \; \alpha \; \alpha \; . \qquad (3.10b)$$

Have you seen the diagrams before? A moment's reflection reveals that the conditions are curvy variants of the axioms for Eilenberg–Moore algebras, (3.8a) and (3.8b), where objects and arrows are replaced by functors and natural transformations. As a result, the diagrams are genuinely dichromatic now. The gray region that is reserved for the terminal category has turned into a colorful one; the corresponding category is called the *source of the action*. Admittedly, the curvy diagrams look like one-sided versions of the monad laws – but this view is less instructive. While other artistic choices have merits, we have adopted the same drawing style, as it allows us to seamlessly combine monad and action laws.

There are also *right actions*, which are the horizontal duals of left actions; see Section 5.4. In this section we deal, however, exclusively with left actions, which is why we mostly drop the qualifier "left" in what follows. We will also say M-action when we wish to be specific about the monad involved.

We also have occasion to consider actions where M is a mere endofunctor F. Such an action is a functor A : $\mathcal{B} \to \mathcal{C}$ and an ordinary natural transformation $\alpha : F \circ A \dot{\to} A$, and is referred to as a *vanilla action*.

Example 3.27. The multiplication $\mu : M \circ M \dot{\to} M$ is both a left and a right action of M. A trivial action, but a useful one. □

Given an action $\alpha : M \circ A \dot{\to} A$, we can form new actions either by placing a dot on the left prong or by outlining the right edge:

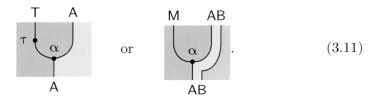

$$\text{(3.11)}$$

Straightforward graphical calculations show that the composite on the right is indeed an action. To be able to establish the coherence conditions for the composite on the left, the dot has to commute with unit and multiplication. In other words, $\tau : T \dot{\to} M$ must be a monad map. The proof then proceeds as follows:

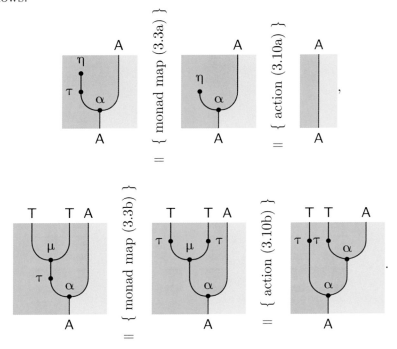

F-algebra	vanilla F-action/natural F-algebra
$(A : \mathcal{C}, a : F\,A \to A)$	$(A : \mathcal{B} \to \mathcal{C}, \alpha : F {\circ} A \dot\to A)$
algebra for M	left action of M/natural algebra for M
$(A : \mathcal{C}, a : M\,A \to A)$	$(A : \mathcal{B} \to \mathcal{C}, \alpha : M {\circ} A \dot\to A)$
homomorphism	transformation of actions/natural homomorphism
$h : (A, a) \to (B, b)$	$h : (A, \alpha) \to (B, \beta)$

Figure 3.3 Relating algebras and actions.

Given a pair of actions of the *same* monad and from the *same* source, a *transformation of actions*, written $h : (A, \alpha) \to (B, \beta)$, is a natural transformation $h : A \dot\to B$ such that the *right turn axiom* holds:

$$\tag{3.12}$$

Sliding the transformation up, it turns into the right branch, tracing the boundary of the source of the action. The law is a curvy variant of the homomorphism axiom (3.6), where objects and arrows are again replaced by functors and natural transformations. Admittedly, the equation looks like a one-sided version of the second monad map axiom (3.3b) – but again, this view is less instructive.

The identity is a transformation of actions, and furthermore transformations compose. So actions of a monad M from the source $\mathcal{B}$ and transformations between them form a category, denoted M-**Act**$(\mathcal{B})$. In a sense, an action can be seen as a "natural" Eilenberg–Moore algebra. Indeed, there is a one-to-one correspondence between actions and functors of type $\mathcal{B} \to \mathcal{C}^{\mathsf{M}}$. Moreover, we have an isomorphism of categories:

$$\mathsf{M}\text{-}\mathbf{Act}(\mathcal{B}) \cong (\mathcal{C}^{\mathsf{M}})^{\mathcal{B}}. \tag{3.13}$$

Exercise 3.22 asks you to fill in the details. It is also possible to define more general mappings between actions; this is explored in Exercise 3.23.

Remark 3.28. We can think of actions and vanilla actions as generalizations of Eilenberg–Moore algebras and algebras for an endofunctor respectively; see Figure 3.3. This is an important idea, since many relationships extend smoothly from algebras to actions once we take this perspective. We will see this idea in practice in Section 5.3.   □

3.6.2 Compatible Actions. Now assume that $A := T$ is a monad, as well – so, we return to monochromatic diagrams. In this case we can also place a lollipop or a fork on the right prong of an action. Then

$$\tag{3.14}$$

is a monad map of type $M \to T$, if the *pseudo-associativity equation*,

$$\tag{3.15}$$

holds. If this is the case, then α is called a *compatible action*. We will also say M-action α is compatible with T, or α is a T-compatible M-action, when we wish to be more specific about the types involved. The property states that the multiplication is a transformation of actions, $\mu : (T \circ T, \alpha \circ T) \dot{\to} (T, \alpha)$. We will also need to refer to vanilla actions that satisfy (3.15), terming them *compatible vanilla actions*.

Turning to the proof, it is straightforward to show that the composite preserves the unit (3.3a):

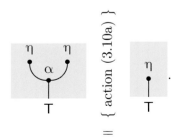

To show that it also preserves multiplication (3.3b), we first invoke the pseudo-associative law (3.15):

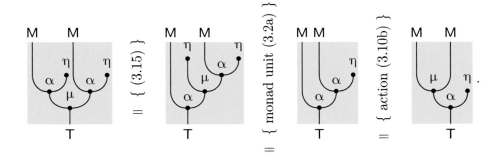

Conversely, given a monad map $\tau : M \dashrightarrow T$, we can construct a compatible action by placing a fork at the bottom:

That the composite is compatible is a consequence of the fact that multiplication is associative (3.2b). Moreover, going round in a circle gives the original gadget: the mappings

$$\alpha \mapsto \quad\quad\quad \tau \mapsto \quad\quad\quad\quad\quad\quad\quad (3.16)$$

establish a one-to-one correspondence between M-actions compatible with T and monad maps $M \dashrightarrow T$. This correspondence turns out to be a useful source of monad maps, as we shall see in Section 5.3.4. There is also a bijective correspondence between vanilla M-actions compatible with T and ordinary natural transformations of type $M \dashrightarrow T$. The proof is entirely analogous to the previous argument for monad actions.

Summary

A monad consists of a functor $\mathsf{M} : \mathcal{C} \to \mathcal{C}$ and natural transformations:

and

Monads on $\mathcal{C}$ and monad maps between them form the category $\mathbf{Mnd}(\mathcal{C})$.

A monad can variably be seen as a mechanism that models side effects in computations or as a device for capturing algebraic theories.

The computer scientist's view is amplified by Kleisli categories, the home of effectful computations. Many familiar categories are isomorphic to Kleisli categories: $\mathbf{Par} \cong \mathbf{Set}_{\mathsf{Maybe}}$ and $\mathbf{Rel} \cong \mathbf{Set}_{\mathsf{Pow}}$.

The algebraist's view is amplified by Eilenberg–Moore categories, the category of algebras for a monad and algebra homomorphisms. Many familiar categories are isomorphic to Eilenberg–Moore categories: $\mathbf{Mon} \cong \mathbf{Set}^{\mathsf{List}}$ and $\mathbf{Sup} \cong \mathbf{Set}^{\mathsf{Pow}}$.

There is also a less restrictive notion of algebra for a mere endofunctor F. These also form a category $\mathsf{F}\text{-}\mathbf{Alg}(\mathcal{C})$.

Monads dualize to comonads with accompanying notions of Co-Kleisli and Co-Eilenberg–Moore categories.

Monad actions generalize the notion of Eilenberg–Moore algebra, and vanilla actions generalize the notion of algebra for an endofunctor.

In this chapter, our diagrams have primarily been monochrome, as we only work with a single category. In fact, our diagrams look like the colorless diagrams used for calculations in a monoidal category. This is not a coincidence, as monoidal categories are exactly the one object bicategories, rendering the use of color redundant.

Further Reading

Monads were introduced by Godement (1964) under the name standard constructions. Kleisli and Eilenberg–Moore categories were introduced in Kleisli (1965) and Eilenberg and Moore (1965) respectively. A single consolidated account of monad theory is somewhat lacking in the existing literature, probably the standard textbook reference is the aging Barr and Wells (2005).

Monads have established themselves as key tools in computer science, program semantics (Moggi, 1991), and the structuring of functional programs (Wadler, 1995).

Graphical aspects of monad theory appeared in Hinze and Marsden (2016a).
A computer science-oriented perspective on monad actions was presented
in Piróg et al. (2015).

Exercises

3.1   ○ Summarize the contents of this chapter in your own words.

3.2   ◉ Show that any pair of diagrams from n inputs to one output built
      out of η and μ are equal; see also Exercise 2.15. Thus, we can use an
      n-dent or an n-pronged fork of type $\mathsf{M}^n \dashrightarrow \mathsf{M}$ as a shorthand for any
      of these diagrams. Does this also hold for diagrams from m inputs to
      n outputs?

3.3   ☉ Confirm that the covariant powerset functor, with the singleton
      and union maps described in Example 3.3, satisfies the monad axioms.
      There is no contravariant powerset monad; why?

3.4   ◉ Fill in the remaining details for the exception monad of Example 3.5,
      and confirm the monad axioms.

3.5   ◉ Let S be a commutative semiring and let $\varphi : X \to \mathsf{S}$ be a function.
      The support of φ is the set of arguments with nonzero image:

$$support\,\varphi := \{\, x \in X \mid \varphi\, x \neq 0 \,\}.$$

Show that $\mathsf{P} : \mathbf{Set} \to \mathbf{Set}$ defined as

$$\mathsf{P}\, X := \{\, \varphi : X \to \mathsf{S} \mid support\,\varphi \text{ is finite}\,\}$$

is a monad. Popular choices for the commutative semiring include $\mathbb{B}$,
$\mathbb{N}$, $\mathbb{Z}$, $\mathbb{Q}$, and $\mathbb{R}$. Which monad is obtained in each case?

3.6   ◉ Let $\mathsf{P}\, A := A \times A$. How many ways are there to turn P into a monad?
      What about $\mathsf{S}\, A := A + A$? Assume that you are working in $\mathbf{Set}$. *Hint:*
      solve Exercise 1.27 first.

3.7   ◉ Show that a monad multiplication μ is a natural isomorphism if and
      only if $\mathsf{M}\circ\eta = \eta\circ\mathsf{M}$, preferably using string diagrams.

3.8   ◉ Show that the following definition of monads is equivalent to the one
      given in Section 3.1:

Let $\mathcal{C}$ be a category. A *monad* over $\mathcal{C}$ consists of an object map
$\mathsf{M} : \mathcal{C} \to \mathcal{C}$, a transformation $\rho\, A : A \to \mathsf{M}\, A$, and a function $(-)^\dagger$ that
extends an arrow $f : A \to \mathsf{M}\, B$ to an arrow $f^\dagger : \mathsf{M}\, A \to \mathsf{M}\, B$, subject to

the following conditions:

$$f^\dagger \cdot \rho\, A = f, \tag{3.17a}$$

$$(\rho\, A)^\dagger = id_{\mathsf{M}\,A}, \tag{3.17b}$$

$$(g^\dagger \cdot f)^\dagger = g^\dagger \cdot f^\dagger. \tag{3.17c}$$

This definition is also known as the *extension form*.

3.9 ⊙ Continuing Exercise 3.8, show that the three conditions (3.17a), (3.17b), and (3.17c) can be written as an equivalence:

$$f = g^\dagger \quad \Longleftrightarrow \quad f \cdot \rho\, A = g, \tag{3.18}$$

for all $f : \mathsf{M}\, A \to \mathsf{M}\, B$ with $f^\dagger = f \cdot id^\dagger$ and for all $g : A \to \mathsf{M}\, B$.

3.10 ⊙ Develop a small graphical calculus to establish the statement of Exercise 3.8. *Hint*: the transformation $\rho\, A$ can be drawn as an edge; to represent $f^\dagger$ we put a box around f.

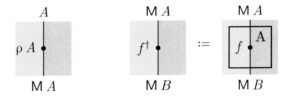

Observe that the edge crossing the upper boundary features a type change. Do you see why $\mathsf{M}\, A$ is *not* represented by two edges?

3.11 ⊙ We saw that nonempty lists form a comonad in Example 3.14. Does the functor List also form a comonad?

3.12 ⊙ Continuing Exercise 3.6, how many ways are there to turn P and S into comonads?

3.13 ⊙ Use string diagrams to show that a monad map $\tau : \mathsf{S} \dot\to \mathsf{T}$ induces a functor $\mathcal{C}_\mathsf{S} \to \mathcal{C}_\mathsf{T}$ between Kleisli categories, whose arrow map is defined $f \mapsto \tau\, B \cdot f$.

3.14 ⊙ What is the Kleisli category of a preorder category?

3.15 ⊙ Define the co-Kleisli category ${}_\mathsf{N}\mathcal{C}$ of a comonad N by dualizing the construction for monads. On a historical note, the construction in Kleisli's seminal paper (Kleisli, 1965) is actually couched in terms of comonads, not monads.

3.16 ⊙ Use string diagrams to show that a monad map $\tau : \mathsf{T} \dot\to \mathsf{S}$ induces also a functor $\mathcal{C}^\mathsf{S} \to \mathcal{C}^\mathsf{T}$ between Eilenberg–Moore categories, whose object map is defined $(A, a) \mapsto (A, a \cdot \tau\, A)$.

3.17 ⊙ Fill in the necessary details from Example 3.25 to show that there is a functor $\mathbf{Mon} \to \mathbf{Set}^{\mathsf{List}}$. Also show that this functor has an inverse.

3.18 ⊙ What is the Eilenberg–Moore category of a preorder category?

3.19 ⊚ Continuing Exercise 3.6, investigate the Eilenberg–Moore categories of the various monads. To which algebraic structures do they correspond?

3.20 ⊚ Continuing Exercise 3.15, also define the co-Eilenberg–Moore $^N\mathcal{C}$ category of a comonad N.

3.21 ⊚ Show that $c : \mathsf{P} \to \mathsf{P}$ is a closure operator (see Example 3.2) if and only if

$$x \leqslant c\,y \quad \Longleftrightarrow \quad c\,x \leqslant c\,y, \tag{3.19}$$

for all $x, y : \mathsf{P}$. Can you provide a categorical interpretation of the equivalence?

3.22 ⊙ Fill in the details of the isomorphism (3.13). *Hint:* define a functor that extracts the carrier and a natural transformation that extracts the action of an algebra.

3.23 ⊙ Transformation of M-actions as defined in Section 3.6 always go between actions with the same source. Find a more general notion of transformation between M-actions on potentially different bases. Draw diagrams describing any axioms that you require, and show that they can be formed into a category with ordinary transformations of M-actions as a subcategory.

4

Adjunctions

In Chapter 3 our diagrams were mostly monochrome, because monads only involve a single category. Adjunctions, the topic of this chapter, relate two categories, and therefore we will return to more colorful diagrams. We shall find that, like monads, adjunctions have a pleasing diagrammatic formulation.

4.1 Adjunction

Adjoint functors are possibly the central contribution of category theory to the wider world of mathematics. They were originally identified in the work of Kan (1958), and their ubiquity inspired Mac Lane's slogan: "Adjoint functors arise everywhere" (1998). Certainly examples abound:

- Algebraic constructions such as free algebras or the abelianization of groups.
- Key topological concepts, such as the Stone–Čech compactification.
- The order theorists' notion of a Galois connection.
- Key ideas in computer science, such as the Rabin–Scott powerset construction for determinization of automata.
- Logical connectives such as the existential and universal quantifiers.
- The existence of key categorical structures such as limits, colimits, or exponentials.

In fact, almost anywhere a canonical or extremal mathematical object is being constructed, there is probably an adjunction lurking in the background, waiting to be identified.

To span such a large range of phenomena, adjunctions necessarily operate at a very high level of abstraction, and can initially be hard to grasp. To provide some motivation, we begin by considering a natural mathematical question: given a functor $\mathsf{F} : \mathcal{C} \to \mathcal{D}$, is there a way of traveling back in the other direction? One obvious choice would be if F has an inverse, taking us back to where we started:

$$\mathsf{F} \circ \mathsf{F}^\circ = \mathsf{Id} \qquad \text{and} \qquad \mathsf{Id} = \mathsf{F}^\circ \circ \mathsf{F}.$$

This is somewhat set-theoretic thinking, as we are not really exploiting the arrows of our categories in any useful way. Rather than an inverse, a more categorical solution would be to ask for a functor G, such that round trips return to somewhere naturally isomorphic to where we started:

$$\mathsf{F} \circ \mathsf{G} \cong \mathsf{Id} \qquad \text{and} \qquad \mathsf{Id} \cong \mathsf{G} \circ \mathsf{F}.$$

This points the way, but a further step would be to loosen up the requirement that we return to an isomorphic object, but rather that there simply be an arrow between the starting point and endpoint. As arrows have directions, there turns out to be two sensible choices:

$$\mathsf{F} \circ \mathsf{G} \dashrightarrow \mathsf{Id} \qquad \text{and} \qquad \mathsf{Id} \dashrightarrow \mathsf{G} \circ \mathsf{F},$$
$$\mathsf{F} \circ \mathsf{G} \dashleftarrow \mathsf{Id} \qquad \text{and} \qquad \mathsf{Id} \dashleftarrow \mathsf{G} \circ \mathsf{F}.$$

This line of thought takes us toward the key aspects of adjunctions. As with every good mathematical concept, there are many different ways to look at adjunctions, and we shall explore the details in this section.

An *adjunction* $\mathsf{L} \dashv \mathsf{R} : \mathcal{C} \rightharpoonup \mathcal{D}$ is often described as a pair of functors $\mathsf{L} : \mathcal{C} \leftarrow \mathcal{D}$ and $\mathsf{R} : \mathcal{C} \to \mathcal{D}$ such that there is a *natural* bijection between collections of arrows:

$$\mathsf{L}\,A \to B : \mathcal{C} \quad \cong \quad A \to \mathsf{R}\,B : \mathcal{D}. \tag{4.1}$$

The functor L is said to be a *left adjoint* for R, while R is L's *right adjoint*. The maps witnessing the bijection, written $\lfloor - \rfloor$ and $\lceil - \rceil$, are called *adjoint transpositions*:

$$\frac{f : \mathsf{L}\,A \to B : \mathcal{C}}{\lfloor f \rfloor : A \to \mathsf{R}\,B : \mathcal{D}} \qquad\qquad \frac{\lceil g \rceil : \mathsf{L}\,A \to B : \mathcal{C}}{g : A \to \mathsf{R}\,B : \mathcal{D}}.$$

The arrow $\lfloor f \rfloor$ is called the *right transpose* of f. Dually, $\lceil g \rceil$ is the *left transpose* of g. That the bijection (4.1) is natural in both A and B means that the following equations hold:

$$\lfloor k \cdot f \cdot \mathsf{L}\,h \rfloor = \mathsf{R}\,k \cdot \lfloor f \rfloor \cdot h, \tag{4.2a}$$
$$k \cdot \lceil g \rceil \cdot \mathsf{L}\,h = \lceil \mathsf{R}\,k \cdot g \cdot h \rceil. \tag{4.2b}$$

Each implies the other, so it is sufficient to establish one of them.

An adjoint situation is often summarized in a diagram like the one shown here:

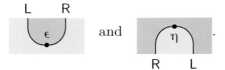

We actually prefer to emphasize an equivalent definition of adjunction that will be more convenient in our graphical calculations. Instead of a natural bijection between two collections of arrows, we require a pair of natural transformations, referred to as the *counit* and *unit* of the adjunction:

Since the adjoint functors L and R involve two categories, the diagrams now feature two colors. The counit $\epsilon : L \circ R \dashrightarrow Id$ resembles a curved cup, the unit $\eta : Id \dashrightarrow R \circ L$ a cap – recall that identity functors are drawn as regions. They are required to satisfy the following *snake equations*, which intuitively allow us to straighten out bends in our string diagrams, by pulling a wire straight:

$$(4.3a) \qquad\qquad (4.3b)$$

More prosaically, the equations identify $L \circ \eta$ and $\eta \circ R$ as split monos, and $\epsilon \circ L$ and $R \circ \epsilon$ as split epis – cut the diagrams horizontally in the middle.

All in all, an adjunction consists of six entities: two functors, two transpositions, and two units. Every single one of these can be defined in terms of the others:

$$\lceil g \rceil = \epsilon\, B \cdot L\, g, \qquad (4.4a)$$
$$\epsilon\, B = \lceil id_{R\,B} \rceil, \qquad (4.4b)$$
$$L\, h = \lceil \eta\, B \cdot h \rceil, \qquad (4.4c)$$

$$\lfloor f \rfloor = R\, f \cdot \eta\, A, \qquad (4.4d)$$
$$\eta\, A = \lfloor id_{L\,A} \rfloor, \qquad (4.4e)$$
$$R\, k = \lfloor k \cdot \epsilon\, A \rfloor. \qquad (4.4f)$$

So, the units are transpositions of the identities. The other formulas are less easy to memorize. They have, however, an appealing visual interpretation, as we shall see in Sections 4.2.2 and 4.6 and later in Section 5.2.

4.1.1 Examples of Adjunctions. We introduce some examples, many of which will recur in later sections. As usual, it pays to consider the simpler case of adjunctions between preorder categories first.

Example 4.1 (Galois Connections). An adjunction between preorder categories is referred to as a *Galois connection*. Concretely, a Galois connection $l \dashv r$ consists of a pair of monotone functions, satisfying the following specialization of (4.1):

$$l\, a \leqslant b \iff a \leqslant r\, b.$$

The assumption that l and r are monotone is actually dispensable, as it follows from the equivalence; see Exercise 4.3.

Recall from Remark 1.3 that a function $f : A \to B$ induces both a direct image function $f^{\blacktriangleright}$, and an inverse image function $f^{\blacktriangleleft}$. They form a Galois connection $f^{\blacktriangleright} \dashv f^{\blacktriangleleft}$, that is,

$$f^{\blacktriangleright} X \subseteq Y \iff X \subseteq f^{\blacktriangleleft} Y.$$

Another example is provided by integer division:

$$m \cdot d \leqslant n \iff m \leqslant n / d,$$

which specifies "/" for positive divisors $d > 0$. (This example motivates our notational choices for Kan extensions in ESD Chapter 6.)

Further examples are provided by least and greatest element (see Example 1.9), meet and join (see Example 1.12), and "implication" (see Example 1.14). The reader is encouraged to carefully spell out the details of the Galois connections; in particular, the preorders involved. □

Example 4.2 (Diagonal Functor). In **Set**, functions to a product are in one-to-one correspondence to pairs of functions from a common source to the components of the product. Dually, functions from a coproduct are in one-to-one correspondence to pairs of functions from the components of the coproduct to a common target. Recall that pairs of arrows live in a product category:

$$(A, A) \to (B_1, B_2) \quad \cong \quad A \to B_1 \times B_2, \tag{4.5a}$$
$$A_1 + A_2 \to B \quad \cong \quad (A_1, A_2) \to (B, B). \tag{4.5b}$$

This almost looks like two adjoint situations. To be able to clearly identify the adjoint functors, it is helpful to rewrite the equivalences using the diagonal functor of Example 1.18, additionally setting $\mathbf{A} := (A_1, A_2)$ and

$\mathbf{B} := (B_1, B_2)$:

$$\Delta\, A \to \mathbf{B} \quad \cong \quad A \to (\times)\, \mathbf{B},$$
$$(+)\, \mathbf{A} \to B \quad \cong \quad \mathbf{A} \to \Delta\, B.$$

So, the diagonal functor has both a left and a right adjoint:

$$\mathbf{Set} \; \underset{\Delta}{\overset{+}{\rightleftarrows}} \; \mathbf{Set}^2 \; \underset{\times}{\overset{\Delta}{\rightleftarrows}} \; \mathbf{Set} \; .$$

Turning to the data of the adjunctions, the counit of $\Delta \dashv (\times)$ is the pair (*outl*, *outr*) of projection functions, and the right transposition is the split operator $-\vartriangle =.$[1] Dually, the unit of $(+) \dashv \Delta$ is the pair of injection functions (*inl*, *inr*), and the left transposition is the join operator $- \triangledown =$.

Abstracting away from the category of sets, we say that the category $\mathcal{C}$ has products (coproducts) if the diagonal functor $\Delta : \mathcal{C} \to \mathcal{C} \times \mathcal{C}$ has a right (left) adjoint. Thus, a boring functor such as the diagonal functor gives rise to two interesting concepts: products and coproducts. Specialized to preorders, products are meets and coproducts are joins; see Example 1.12. Compare equivalences (1.9a)–(1.9b) to (4.5a)–(4.5b). □

Example 4.3 (Currying). In Examples 3.6 and 3.15 we described the state monad and the costate comonad, using products and exponentials. In fact, these two constructions are related by an adjunction:

$$\mathbf{Set} \; \underset{(-)^P}{\overset{-\times P}{\rightleftarrows}} \; \mathbf{Set} \; .$$

In **Set** a function of two arguments can be treated as a function of the first argument that returns a function of the second argument:

$$A \times P \to B \quad \cong \quad A \to B^P.$$

The left adjoint of the curry adjunction is $\mathsf{L}\, A := A \times P$, its right adjoint is $\mathsf{R}\, B = B^X$. The right transposition is currying, Λf; the left transposition, uncurrying. The counit of the curry adjunction is function application, $apply\, B : B^X \times X \to B$; its unit $\eta\, A : A \to (A \times P)^P$ coincides with the unit of the state monad. This is, of course, not a coincidence, as we shall see in Section 5.1.

Abstracting away from **Set**, we say that the category $\mathcal{C}$ has exponentials if $- \times P$ has a right adjoint for every object P. In this case, $(=)^{(-)}$ can be

---

[1] Do not confuse the diagonal functor Δ, the Greek letter delta, with the split operator $\vartriangle$, an upwards pointing triangle.

turned into a bifunctor of type $\mathcal{C}^{\mathrm{op}} \times \mathcal{C} \to \mathcal{C}$. Observe that the parameter P appears in a contravariant position. (Do you see why?)   □

A category is called *Cartesian closed* if it has final objects, products, and exponentials. Cartesian closed categories can be used to give a semantics to the simply typed lambda calculus.

Example 4.4 (Relations). Continuing Example 3.19, there is an identity on objects functor $\mathsf{J} : \mathbf{Set} \to \mathbf{Rel}$ sending a function $f : X \to Y$ to its *graph*:

$$\mathsf{J}f := \{\,(x, y) \mid f\,x = y\,\}.$$

(If you like to think of functions as "simple" and "entire" relations, then J is an inclusion functor.) This functor has a right adjoint sending each relation $R : X \to Y$ to its *extension* to powersets $\mathsf{E}\,R : \mathcal{P}\,X \to \mathcal{P}\,Y$:

$$\mathsf{E}\,R := \lambda\,U\,.\,\{\,v \mid \exists u \in U\,.\,u\,R\,v\,\}.$$

Turning to the data of the adjunction,

$$\mathbf{Rel} \underset{\mathsf{E}}{\overset{\mathsf{J}}{\xleftrightarrows{\;\perp\;}}} \mathbf{Set},$$

the unit is the *function* that maps an element to a singleton set; its counit $\epsilon\,B : \mathcal{P}\,B \to B$ is the *relation* that relates a set U to an element u if and only if $U \ni u$. (The right transpose is sometimes written $\Lambda\,R$, clashing with the notation for the right transpose of the curry adjunction.)   □

Example 4.5 (Free Monoids). Example 1.22 introduced the forgetful functor $\mathsf{U} : \mathbf{Mon} \to \mathbf{Set}$, which sends each monoid $(A, e, \bullet)$ to its underlying set A, and the free functor $\mathsf{Free} : \mathbf{Set} \to \mathbf{Mon}$, which sends a set A to the free monoid over A, $(\mathsf{List}\,A, [\,], +\!\!+)$. They are part of an adjoint situation:

$$\mathbf{Mon} \underset{\mathsf{U}}{\overset{\mathsf{Free}}{\xleftrightarrows{\;\perp\;}}} \mathbf{Set}\ .$$

The counit of the adjunction $\mathsf{Free} \dashv \mathsf{U}$ is the *monoid homomorphism reduce* introduced in Example 1.28, which reduces a list to a single element. The unit is the *function* that maps an element to the singleton list. Again, a boring functor, the forgetful functor, gives rise to an interesting concept, the free construction.   □

4.2 Reasoning with Adjunctions

4.2.1 Uniqueness of Adjoints.
Let us illustrate the use of the snake equations by proving an important result about adjoint functors. The right ad-

joint of a functor, if it exists, is unique up to natural isomorphism. Let $L_1 \dashv R_1, L_2 \dashv R_2 : \mathcal{C} \to \mathcal{D}$ be two parallel adjunctions. Then

$$L_1 \cong L_2 \iff R_1 \cong R_2. \tag{4.6}$$

We show the left-to-right direction; the other direction has a symmetric proof. If σ witnesses the isomorphism of the left adjoints, then the natural isomorphism for the right adjoints is given by two "fake" snakes:

and

If we compose the two "fake" snakes vertically, so that one snake bites the other snake's tail, we can pull the entire string straight using applications of the snake equations (4.3a) and (4.3b) and the assumption that σ is an isomorphism:

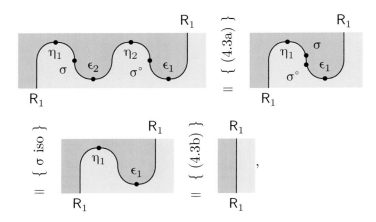

and in the other direction:

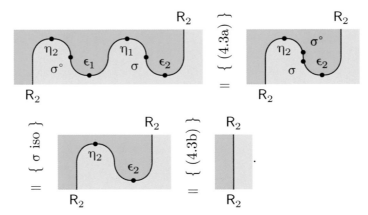

Therefore, if $L \dashv R_1$ and $L \dashv R_2$, then $R_1 \cong R_2$, and dually, if $L_1 \dashv R$ and $L_2 \dashv R$, then $L_1 \cong L_2$, so "adjoints are unique up to isomorphism."

4.2.2 Back to Bijections. Using the units of an adjunction, we can also express the natural bijection (4.1) as an equivalence:

$$\tag{4.7}$$

The equivalence is established by "bending wires," where a double bend is pulled straight using the snake equations (4.3a) and (4.3b). For example, for the left-to-right direction we place a cap on L, bending the functor down to the left, turning it into an R – an arm is turned into a leg! So the transpositions are wire-bending operations – this is the promised diagrammatic reading of (4.4a) and (4.4d).

If the arrows f and g are related by the adjunction $L \dashv R$, that is, by either side of (4.7), then we write $f \, (L \dashv R) \, g$. If $L \dashv R$ is obvious from the context, we abbreviate $f \, (L \dashv R) \, g$ by $f \dashv g$, pictorially:

$$\tag{4.8}$$

Quite pleasingly, the diagrams provide the necessary type information. That the bijection is natural in A and B has an appealing visual interpretation: relation (4.8) is invariant under placing "beads" on the A and B wires:

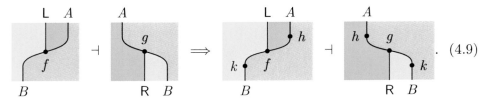

$$(4.9)$$

Bending the L and R wires simply does not affect the A and B wires. Observe that because of the bending, $L\,h$ and k on the left turn into h and $R\,k$ on the right. Thus, placing a "bead" on the A wire corresponds to precomposing with $L\,h$ or h. Dually, placing a "bead" on the B wire corresponds to postcomposing with k or $R\,k$.

The notion of an adjunction, like every other worthwhile concept, enjoys several complementary definitions. We have touched upon one approach, an adjunction as a natural bijection between sets of arrows, and elaborated a second one, the definition in terms of the units. Each view comes equipped with specific proof techniques. Bending wires is the technique of choice for the second view. The first view is useful if we want to speak about the arrows *related* by an adjunction in tandem. This gives rise to an important proof principle that we shall explore in Section 4.4 and ESD Chapter 5 – the implication (4.9) is a first taste. The relational style often avoids asymmetric arguments that are typical of a functional style.

4.2.3 Lifting Adjunctions to Functor Categories. If we examine Equivalence (4.7), we observe that the correspondence remains valid if we replace the objects A and B by functors and the arrows f and g by natural transformations:

$$(4.10a)$$

Since A and B are functors, the diagrams feature one additional color. Equivalence (4.10a) establishes a one-to-one correspondence between natural transformations of type $L \circ A \xrightarrow{\cdot} B$ and natural transformations of type

$A \dashrightarrow R \circ B$, which is natural in A and B. In other words, precomposition with L is left adjoint to precomposition with R.

In the diagrams above we have operated to the left of A and B. Bending the wires works equally well on the right:

$$\begin{array}{ccccccc} \text{A R} & & \text{A R} & & \text{A} & & \text{A} \\ & = & & \Longleftrightarrow & & = & \\ \text{B} & & \text{B} & & \text{B L} & & \text{B L} \end{array} \qquad (4.10\text{b})$$

Equivalence (4.10b) establishes a one-to-one correspondence between natural transformations of type $A \circ R \dashrightarrow B$ and natural transformations of type $A \dashrightarrow B \circ L$, which is natural in A and B. In other words, postcomposition with R is left adjoint to postcomposition with L. The diagrams are rotations of the previous ones: precomposition is turned into postcomposition. (The colors do not quite match up, as the universally quantified variables A and B have different types in each case, while the types of L and R are fixed.)

To summarize, every adjunction $L \dashv R$ induces two adjunctions between functor categories: $L \circ - \dashv R \circ -$ and $- \circ R \dashv - \circ L$.

$$L \circ A \dashrightarrow B \;\cong\; A \dashrightarrow R \circ B \qquad \text{and} \qquad A \circ R \dashrightarrow B \;\cong\; A \dashrightarrow B \circ L \qquad (4.11)$$

Just in case you are wondering, the units of these adjunctions are also given by precompositions, $\epsilon \circ -$ and $\eta \circ -$, and postcompositions, $- \circ \epsilon$ and $- \circ \eta$, which are higher-order natural transformations.

4.3 Composition of Adjunctions

A distinctive feature of adjunctions is that they compose nicely, as can be seen from the following diagrams for the counits and units. A pair of adjunctions with units and counits,

can be composed to form a new adjunction, by nesting the counits and units, as suggested by the colors of the regions:

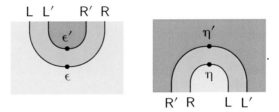

Like Matryoshka dolls, the natural transformations are placed one inside the other. Because of the nesting, the left and right adjoints are composed in different orders: the composition of $L \dashv R$ and $L' \dashv R'$ gives $L{\circ}L' \dashv R'{\circ}R$. Using the sweep-line algorithm we can easily read off the symbolic notation of the units: $\epsilon \cdot (L{\circ}\epsilon'{\circ}R)$ and $(R'{\circ}\eta{\circ}L') \cdot \eta'$.

The snake equations follow from the original adjunctions as follows:

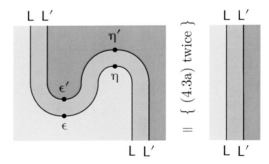

and

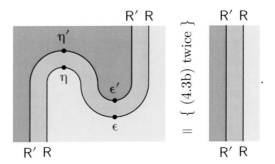

Nested cups and caps give rise to parallel snakes, which can be pulled straight in parallel. (Well, do not take this too literally.) Contrast the diagrams to the algebraic formulation:

$$(\epsilon \circ L \circ L') \cdot (L \circ \epsilon' \circ R \circ L \circ L') \cdot (L \circ L' \circ R' \circ \eta \circ L') \cdot (L \circ L' \circ \eta') = L \circ L',$$
$$(R' \circ R \circ \epsilon) \cdot (R' \circ R \circ L \circ \epsilon' \circ R) \cdot (R' \circ \eta \circ L' \circ R' \circ R) \cdot (\eta' \circ R' \circ R) = R' \circ R.$$

You are encouraged, or perhaps you are discouraged, to redo the proofs using the symbolic notation.

Henceforth, when dealing with multiple adjunctions, we overload the letters ϵ and η for the counits and units of the adjunctions. The type information in the diagrams should resolve any ambiguity about which natural transformations are intended.

Example 4.6. A *regular algebra* or *quantale* is a complete join-semilattice with a monoid structure that distributes over the joins. Given these two components, it is perhaps unsurprising that we can break the free quantale construction into two steps, first adding the monoid structure, and then extending it with join-semilattice structure:

$$\mathbf{Reg} \xleftarrow[U]{\overset{Free}{\underset{\perp}{\longleftarrow}}} \mathbf{Mon} \xleftarrow[U]{\overset{Free}{\underset{\perp}{\longleftarrow}}} \mathbf{Set} \ .$$

We saw the free monoid construction in Example 4.5. In the second stage, Free : **Mon** → **Reg** sends the underlying set of a monoid to its powerset and extends the monoid structure to subsets as follows:

$$E := \{\, e \,\} \qquad \text{and} \qquad U \bullet V := \{\, u \bullet v \mid u \in U, v \in V \,\}. \tag{4.12}$$

The two right adjoints are underlying functors: U : **Reg** → **Mon** forgets about the semilattice structure, retaining the monoid structure; U : **Mon** → **Set** forgets about the latter (1.13).   □

4.4 Mates

Next, we introduce a simple but powerful proof technique.

A natural transformation relates two parallel functors. Similarly, a compatible pair of natural transformations relates two parallel adjunctions. Given $L \dashv R, L' \dashv R' : \mathcal{C} \to \mathcal{D}$, the natural transformations $\sigma : L' \dot{\to} L$ and $\tau : R \dot{\to} R'$ are *mates*, $(\sigma \dashv \tau) : (L \dashv R) \to (L' \dashv R') : \mathcal{C} \to \mathcal{D}$, pictorially:

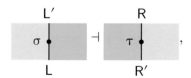

,

provided the following conditions hold:

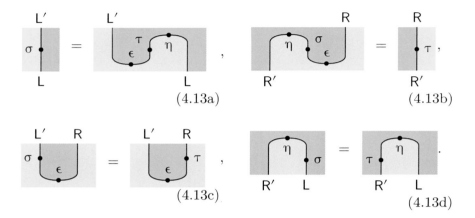

(4.13a)   (4.13b)

(4.13c)   (4.13d)

Observe that σ maps L′ to L, whereas τ maps R to R′ – this is because left adjoints appear in a contravariant position in the bijection of arrows,

$$L\,A \to B : \mathcal{C} \quad \cong \quad A \to R\,B : \mathcal{D},$$

whereas right adjoints appear in a covariant position.

Each of the preceding conditions implies the others, as natural transformations of type L′ $\dot{\to}$ L are in one-to-one correspondence to those of type R $\dot{\to}$ R′ (4.11). In particular, one mate uniquely determines the other: given a natural transformation $\sigma : $ L′ $\dot{\to}$ L, there is a *unique* natural transformation $\tau : $ R $\dot{\to}$ R′ so that σ and τ are mates (4.13b), and vice versa (4.13a). This simple fact gives rise to a useful proof principle. Let $(\sigma \dashv \tau), (\sigma' \dashv \tau') : $ (L $\dashv$ R) $\to$ (L′ $\dashv$ R′) be two parallel mates. Then:

$$\sigma = \sigma' \quad \Longleftrightarrow \quad \tau' = \tau. \qquad (4.14)$$

4.4.1 Composition of Mates. Before applying the principle, it is useful to first explore the compositional structure of mates. There is an identity mate:

$$\qquad (4.15)$$

and mates, like natural transformations, can be composed vertically and horizontally. If we have pairs of mates,

we can form their *vertical composition*:

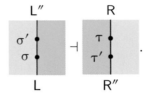

Note that the left and right mates are composed in opposite orders. This is imperative, given their typings. The proof that the composites are mates additionally provides a visual explanation:

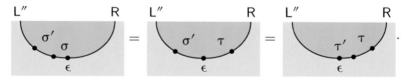

The left mates are moved sequentially to the other side, first σ', then σ. As the vertices are pushed around the base, the order of vertical composition is reversed. Think of shunting a pair of trains out of one depot and into another.

We can also compose pairs of mates horizontally. If the following are pairs of mates,

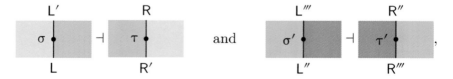

then their *horizontal composition* is a pair of mates, as well:

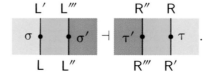

Note that left and right adjoints and hence left and right mates are composed in opposite order. Again, this is a consequence of their typings. And again, the proof of conjugacy provides an intuitive visual explanation:

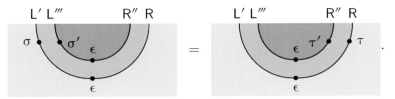

This time, we move σ' and σ in parallel: σ' along the perimeter of the outer cap, σ along the inner cap. Due to the nesting of cups, the order of horizontal composition is reversed.

4.4.2 Reasoning with Mates. To illustrate the technique of "reasoning with mates," let us provide an alternative proof of the fact that adjoint functors are unique up to isomorphism; see Section 4.2.1. Let $(\sigma \dashv \tau) : (L \dashv R) \to (L' \dashv R')$ and $(\sigma' \dashv \tau') : (L' \dashv R') \to (L \dashv R)$ be opposite mates. Instantiating the proof principle (4.14) to the composite mates and to the identity, we immediately obtain

In words, σ is a split epi if and only if τ is a split mono, and dually. Joining the two equivalences we obtain the desired result:

$$\sigma : L' \cong L \iff \tau : R \cong R'. \tag{4.16}$$

While the original proof was elementary, this higher-level proof is short and sweet.

Horizontal and vertical composition of mates can be seen as proof rules that allow us to relate two natural transformations. In Section 4.2.1 we have discussed rules for relating arrows. Joining the two threads, the following law combines mated arrows and mated natural transformations. If $f \dashv g$ and $\sigma \dashv \tau$, represented pictorially as follows:

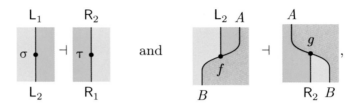

then

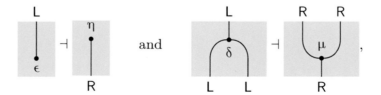

(4.17)

While Rule (4.9) enabled us to manipulate the A and B wires, the preceding rule (4.17) operates on the L and R wires. We discuss an application in the next section, which provides further evidence for the economy of reasoning afforded by mates.

4.5 Adjoint Comonads and Monads

Assume that a left adjoint is at the same time a comonad. Then its right adjoint is a monad! Dually, the left adjoint of a monad, if it exists, is a comonad. A symmetric description is this: for adjoint endofunctors $\mathsf{L} \dashv \mathsf{R} :$ $\mathcal{C} \to \mathcal{C}$ and pairs of mates

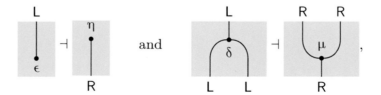

we have

$$\mathsf{L} \text{ comonad} \quad \Longleftrightarrow \quad \mathsf{R} \text{ monad}. \tag{4.18}$$

If either side of the equivalence holds, we write $(\mathsf{L}, \epsilon, \delta) \dashv (\mathsf{R}, \eta, \mu)$. To establish (4.18) we have to show that the comonadic laws imply the monadic laws and vice versa. Instantiating (4.14) to the ingredients of counit, unit, coassociative, and associative laws, we obtain

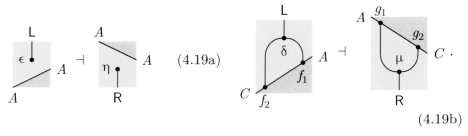

The diagrams on the left are related to the corresponding diagrams on the right by a rotation of 180°. For example, the *first* counit law is related to the *second* unit law; the mates are constructed by horizontal and vertical composition from the assumptions $\epsilon \dashv \eta$, $\delta \dashv \mu$, and $\mathsf{L} \dashv \mathsf{R}$.

Since comonadic programs of type $\mathsf{L}\, A \to B$ are in one-to-one correspondence to monadic programs of type $A \to \mathsf{R}\, B$, it stands to reason that the co-Kleisli category of L (see Exercise 3.15) is isomorphic to the Kleisli category of R. In other words, the one-to-one correspondence preserves identities and composition of Kleisli arrows, represented pictorially as follows:

The mates are constructed by applying Rule (4.17) to the various assumptions: $\epsilon \dashv \eta$, $\delta \dashv \mu$, $A \dashv A$, $f_1 \dashv g_1$, and $f_2 \dashv g_2$. Two remarks are in order. The diagrams for counit and unit involve the identity adjunction $\mathsf{Id} \dashv \mathsf{Id}$. Correspondingly, $A \dashv A$ expands to id_A ($\mathsf{Id} \dashv \mathsf{Id}$) id_A. The diagrams for comultiplication and multiplication involve the composite adjunction $L \circ L \dashv R \circ R$. An explicit proof that the two "staircases"

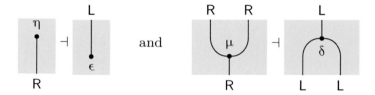

$$(4.20)$$

are related involves the nested units of composite adjunctions, the Matryoshka dolls (see Section 4.3) and is left as Exercise 4.12.

Example 4.7. The curry adjunction provides an example where the left adjoint $L := - \times P$ is also a comonad. The so-called *product comonad* provides contextual information, ϵ discards this information, and δ duplicates it. Equivalence (4.18) implies that L's right adjoint $R := (-)^P$ is a monad, commonly known as the *reader* or *environment* monad. The theory confirms our intuition that the product comonad and the reader monad solve the same problem. $\qquad\qquad\square$

We will see another source of monads and comonads forming adjoint pairs in Section 5.1. But first we will need to lay a bit more groundwork.

Just in case you are wondering, the dual situation holds, as well. For adjoint endofunctors $L \dashv R : \mathcal{C} \to \mathcal{C}$ and pairs of mates

we have

$$L \text{ monad} \quad \Longleftrightarrow \quad R \text{ comonad}. \tag{4.21}$$

In this case, the Eilenberg–Moore category of L is isomorphic to the co-Eilenberg–Moore category of R. The details are relegated to Exercise 4.13.

4.6 Reflective and Coreflective Subcategories

By considering properties of the unit and counit, we can derive more information about an adjunction $L \dashv R : \mathcal{C} \to \mathcal{D}$. Firstly, we recall that the arrow maps of adjoint functors can be expressed in terms of the units,

$\mathsf{L}\,h = \lceil \eta\, B \cdot h \rceil$ (4.4c) and $\mathsf{R}\,k = \lfloor k \cdot \epsilon\, A \rfloor$ (4.4f), indicating the transpositions by white boundaries,

$$(4.22)$$

$$(4.23)$$

These are the snake equations with arrows added to the far right. Now we rewrite the characterizations as compositions of arrow maps:

$$\mathsf{L}_{A,B} = \lceil - \rceil \cdot (\eta\, B \cdot -),$$
$$\mathsf{R}_{A,B} = \lfloor - \rfloor \cdot (- \cdot \epsilon\, A).$$

Since the transpositions $\lceil - \rceil$ and $\lfloor - \rfloor$ are isomorphisms, we observe that $\mathsf{L}_{A,B}$ is injective if and only if $\eta\, B \cdot -$ is injective. Recalling that $g \cdot -$ is injective if and only if g is mono (1.6a), we immediately obtain

$$\text{L faithful} \iff \eta\, A \text{ mono for all } A, \tag{4.24a}$$
$$\text{L full} \iff \eta\, A \text{ split epi for all } A, \tag{4.24b}$$
$$\text{R faithful} \iff \epsilon\, B \text{ epi for all } B, \tag{4.24c}$$
$$\text{R full} \iff \epsilon\, B \text{ split mono for all } B. \tag{4.24d}$$

Analogous arguments establish the other equivalences.

If R is fully faithful, then the components of ϵ are both split mono and epi arrows, and are therefore isomorphisms; see Exercise 1.11. Therefore, R is fully faithful if and only if ϵ is a natural isomorphism (2.8). Under these circumstances, $\mathcal{C}$ is called a *reflective subcategory* of $\mathcal{D}$. By duality, L is fully faithful if and only if η is a natural isomorphism, and then $\mathcal{D}$ is described as a *coreflective subcategory* of $\mathcal{C}$.

Example 4.8 (Groups). The category of abelian groups is a reflective subcategory of the category of groups: the inclusion functor **Ab** → **Grp** has a left adjoint, the free construction that "abelianizes" a group (quotienting a group by its commutator subgroup $G/[G, G]$). The category of groups is both a reflective and a coreflective subcategory of the category of monoids: the forgetful functor **Grp** → **Mon** has a left adjoint, the free construction that maps a monoid to the "group of fractions"; it also has a right adjoint, the cofree construction that maps a monoid to its group of invertible elements. □

Fully faithful right adjoints allow us to perform further diagrammatic manoeuvres, popping bubbles and snapping bands of double wires:

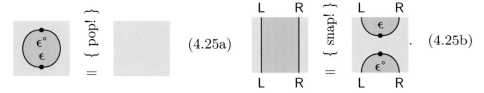

$$(4.25a) \qquad\qquad (4.25b)$$

A dual pair of equations hold for fully faithful left adjoints, for η and η°. Popping a bubble is an obvious simplification step; unpopping a bubble is a not-so-obvious complication step, which is best avoided in favor of more high-level manoeuvres (e.g. "attaching an ear" in Section 4.7.2). Such a calculational move is like pulling a rabbit out of a hat, as bubbles can appear literally everywhere in a diagram.

4.7 Equivalences of Categories

A reflective subcategory features a counit that is a natural isomorphism. Dually, a coreflective subcategory has a unit that is an isomorphism. Picking up a loose thread from the introduction to this chapter, we now consider a perfectly symmetric situation, captured by a pair of natural isomorphisms.

4.7.1 Equivalences. Two categories $\mathcal{C}$ and $\mathcal{D}$ are *equivalent*, written $\mathcal{C} \simeq \mathcal{D}$, if there is a pair of functors $F : \mathcal{C} \to \mathcal{D}$ and $G : \mathcal{C} \leftarrow \mathcal{D}$ and a pair of natural isomorphisms $\alpha : F{\circ}G \cong \mathrm{Id}_{\mathcal{D}}$ and $\beta : G{\circ}F \cong \mathrm{Id}_{\mathcal{C}}$:

We write $\mathsf{F} : \mathcal{C} \simeq \mathcal{D} : \mathsf{G}$, if we wish to name the witnesses F and G. The data is called an *equivalence of categories*.

The relation $\simeq$ is reflexive, symmetric, transitive, and compatible with most constructions on categories. Reflexivity is established by identity functors and identity natural transformations. More generally, isomorphic categories are equivalent. In this case, the natural transformations are identities. The converse is not true; see Example 4.9. Symmetry is shown by reflecting the natural isomorphisms vertically. Transitivity is established by nesting cups and caps like Matryoshka dolls; see Section 4.3. To prove that the nested transformations are isomorphisms, we first pop the inner bubble and then the outer one:

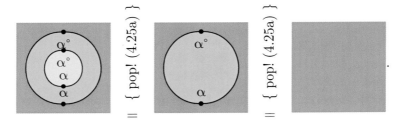

Likewise, for the reverse direction we first snap the inner band and then the outer one:

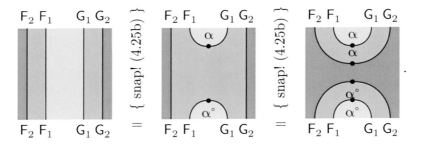

(These calculations can be seen as the two-dimensional counterparts of the proofs in Section 1.2.3, which show that the relation $\cong$ is transitive.)

Equivalence is a better notion of "sameness" for categories, rather than isomorphism, because it incorporates isomorphisms of objects, rather than strict equality.

Example 4.9. The category of finite-dimensional real vector spaces and linear maps is equivalent to the category with objects natural numbers, and arrows $n \to m$ real-valued matrices of dimension $m \times n$; see Exercise 1.3. Intuitively both encode linear algebra, and so should be "the same" from a categorical perspective, but they are *not* isomorphic categories. This is clear from a size argument, as $\mathbb{N}$ is a set, but the collection of finite-dimensional real vector spaces is "too big" to form a set. $\square$

Definition 4.10 (Skeleton). A *skeleton* of a category $\mathcal{C}$ is a full subcategory of $\mathcal{C}$ that contains exactly one representative from each isomorphism class. If we think of isomorphic objects as being essentially the same, they represent a sort of redundancy within a category. A skeleton is then minimal in that all these redundancies are removed.

A category is equivalent, but not necessarily isomorphic, to each of its skeletons. For example **Fin** is equivalent to its full subcategory of finite cardinals, but they are clearly not isomorphic, if we consider the "size" of their collections of objects. $\square$

The previous examples illustrate how equivalence, not isomorphism, is the right notion of "sameness" for categories. The categorically natural properties of categories, such as having a terminal object, products, or exponentials, are carried across equivalences. In fact, we could take that as a definition. From this perspective, categorically unnatural properties are things like having a certain number of objects, or being a skeleton!

Example 4.11 (Duality). A *duality* between two categories $\mathcal{C}$ and $\mathcal{D}$ is an equivalence between $\mathcal{C}$ and $\mathcal{D}^{op}$. Such dualities are an important topic in category theory, often providing surprising connections. Possibly the most famous example is Stone duality (1936; 1937), a duality between **Bool**^{op} and a certain category of topological spaces, referred to as Stone spaces. This result has deep implications in logic, and laid the foundations for a rich line of inquiry.

Many dualities involve similar relationships between algebraic and geometric structures. We discussed preservation and reflection of structure in Remark 1.3. Intuitively, it is the reversal of direction when relating a category with structure-preserving arrows, such as a class of algebras and their homomorphisms, to one with structure-reflecting ones, such as topological spaces and continuous maps, that leads to the characteristic contravariance in duality theory.

As the simplest instance of Stone duality, the category of *finite* Boolean algebras is dual to **Fin**, the category of *finite* sets. The adjoints are given by the contravariant powerset functor and the functor that sends a finite Boolean lattice L to its set of atoms $\mathcal{A}\,L$. The inverse image function $f^{\blacktriangleleft} : \mathcal{P}\,Y \to \mathcal{P}\,X$ is a Boolean homomorphism, as it preserves meet, join, and complement. The counit $\epsilon\,L : \mathcal{P}\,(\mathcal{A}\,L) \cong L$ witnesses the isomorphism between sets of atoms and lattice elements: $\epsilon\,L\,X := \bigsqcup X$ and $\epsilon^{\circ}\,L\,a := \{\,x \in \mathcal{A}\,L \mid x \leqslant a\,\}$. The unit

$\eta X : X \cong \mathcal{A}(\mathcal{P} X)$ witnesses the isomorphism between elements and single-ton sets, the atoms of a powerset lattice: $\eta X x := \{x\}$ and $\eta° X \{x\} := x$.

To illustrate, Boolean homomorphisms of type $2^3 \to 2^2$ are in one-to-one correspondence with functions of type $3 \leftarrow 2$.

$$\text{⬡} \quad \to \quad \text{◇} \quad \cong \quad \bullet\bullet\bullet \quad \leftarrow \quad \bullet\bullet.$$

The atoms are shaded in the diagrams. □

Turning to the properties of an equivalence, the participating functors are fully faithful and essentially bijective. To establish the result, we start recording some immediate properties of the natural isomorphisms:

$$\mathsf{F}\circ\mathsf{G} \cong \mathsf{Id}_{\mathcal{D}} \implies \begin{cases} \mathsf{F}\circ\mathsf{G} \text{ is fully faithful and essentially bijective,} \\ \mathsf{F} \text{ is essentially surjective,} \\ \mathsf{G} \text{ is faithful.} \end{cases}$$

The identity functor $\mathsf{Id}_{\mathcal{D}}$ is fully faithful and essentially bijective. The naturally isomorphic functor $\mathsf{F}\circ\mathsf{G}$ inherits both properties (2.9f). Furthermore, F is essentially surjective and G is faithful; see Exercise 1.32.

A symmetric argument shows that F is faithful and G is essentially surjective. In this situation, we can furthermore conclude that F is essentially injective and G is full:

$$\mathsf{F}\circ\mathsf{G} \cong \mathsf{Id}_{\mathcal{D}} \implies \begin{cases} \mathsf{G} \text{ essentially surjective} \implies \mathsf{F} \text{ essentially injective,} \\ \mathsf{F} \text{ faithful} \implies \mathsf{G} \text{ full.} \end{cases}$$

To establish that F is essentially injective, let $A_1, A_2 : \mathcal{C}$ be arbitrary objects of $\mathcal{C}$. As G is essentially surjective, there are objects $B_1, B_2 : \mathcal{D}$ with $A_1 \cong \mathsf{G} B_1$ and $A_2 \cong \mathsf{G} B_2$. Then

$$\mathsf{F} A_1 \cong \mathsf{F} A_2 \iff \mathsf{F}(\mathsf{G} B_1) \cong \mathsf{F}(\mathsf{G} B_2)$$
$$\iff B_1 \cong B_2 \implies \mathsf{G} B_1 \cong \mathsf{G} B_2 \iff A_1 \cong A_2.$$

To show the fullness of the functor G, we begin with an arbitrary arrow $f : \mathsf{G} A \to \mathsf{G} B$, in pictures:

$$\mathsf{G}\ A$$

$$\mathsf{G}\ B$$

Now we would like to find some $g : A \to B$ such that $\mathsf{G} g = f$. An obvious plan is to start with f, and build a suitable candidate. Diagrammatically, we connect the G-wires of f to a bubble (forming a "speech balloon"):

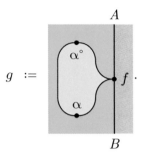

Since F is faithful, it suffices to show $F(Gg) = Ff$. The proof proceeds by first snapping and then unsnapping bands of double wires:

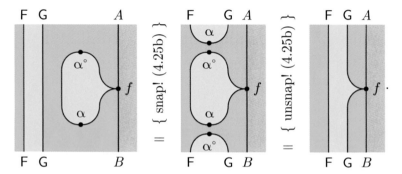

4.7.2 Adjoint Equivalences. The definition of an equivalence is tantalizingly close to that of an adjunction – only the snake equations are missing on the list of requirements. So, it probably comes as no surprise that an equivalence induces an *adjoint equivalence*:

$$F : \mathcal{C} \simeq \mathcal{D} : G \quad \Longleftrightarrow \quad F \dashv G : \mathcal{C} \simeq \mathcal{D}, \tag{4.26}$$

where $F \dashv G : \mathcal{C} \simeq \mathcal{D}$ denotes an adjunction whose units are natural isomorphisms. Since $\simeq$ is symmetric, actually two adjoint equivalences are induced: $F \dashv G$ and $G \dashv F$.

Remark 4.12. The logical equivalence (4.26) shows that to show two categories are adjoint equivalent, it is sufficient to establish they are simply equivalent.

It is tempting to look for other weaker conditions for equivalence. One plausible candidate is to consider a functor F, with both left and right adjoints $L \dashv F \dashv R$. This situation occurs regularly in practice, and certainly doesn't imply F is an equivalence. What if we also require $L = R$?

In fact, this is still not sufficient for F to be an equivalence. Consider, for example, the terminal category $\mathbf{1}$. The unique functor $\mathcal{D} \to \mathbf{1}$ has a left adjoint $\mathsf{L} : \mathbf{1} \to \mathcal{D}$ if and only if $\mathcal{D}$ has an initial object, and a right adjoint $\mathsf{R} : \mathbf{1} \to \mathcal{D}$ if and only if $\mathcal{D}$ has a terminal object. If $\mathcal{D}$ is a category with a zero object, so that the initial and terminal objects coincide, then $\mathsf{L} = \mathsf{R}$. This is the case, for example, for $\mathbf{Rel}$, where the empty set is the zero object, but it is not the case that $\mathbf{Rel}$ is equivalent to $\mathbf{1}$. $\qquad\square$

The right-to-left direction of (4.26) holds by definition. To establish the left-to-right direction we remind ourselves that the functors of an equivalence are fully faithful, and reason thus:

$$
\begin{aligned}
&\mathsf{F}\,A \to B \\
\cong\ & \{\ \mathsf{G}\text{ is fully faithful (1.19) }\} \\
&\mathsf{G}\,(\mathsf{F}\,A) \to \mathsf{G}\,B \\
\cong\ & \{\ \beta : \mathsf{G}{\circ}\mathsf{F} \cong \mathsf{Id}_{\mathcal{C}}\ \} \\
&A \to \mathsf{G}\,B.
\end{aligned}
$$

The bijection between collections of arrows is natural in both A and B, as required. Interestingly, the preceding proof uses only a part of the given data. Indeed, we can conduct four analogous proofs to obtain

$$
\begin{aligned}
\mathsf{F} \dashv \mathsf{G} \quad & \begin{cases} \mathsf{F}\,A \to B \cong \mathsf{G}\,(\mathsf{F}\,A) \to \mathsf{G}\,B \cong A \to \mathsf{G}\,B, \\ \mathsf{F}\,A \to B \cong \mathsf{F}\,A \to \mathsf{F}\,(\mathsf{G}\,B) \cong A \to \mathsf{G}\,B, \end{cases} \\[2mm]
\mathsf{G} \dashv \mathsf{F} \quad & \begin{cases} \mathsf{G}\,A \to B \cong \mathsf{F}\,(\mathsf{G}\,A) \to \mathsf{F}\,B \cong A \to \mathsf{F}\,B, \\ \mathsf{G}\,A \to B \cong \mathsf{G}\,A \to \mathsf{G}\,(\mathsf{F}\,B) \cong A \to \mathsf{F}\,B. \end{cases}
\end{aligned}
$$

So an equivalence actually induces *four* adjunctions! In general, the two adjunctions that establish F as a left adjoint are different, and likewise for G. In particular, it is generally not the case that $\alpha : \mathsf{F}{\circ}\mathsf{G} \cong \mathsf{Id}_{\mathcal{D}}$ is the counit of $\mathsf{F} \dashv \mathsf{G}$ with $\beta^{\circ} : \mathsf{Id}_{\mathcal{C}} \cong \mathsf{G}{\circ}\mathsf{F}$ acting as the unit. In contrast to the units of an adjunction, the two isomorphisms of an equivalence are completely unrelated; see Exercise 4.18.

This situation clearly warrants further investigation. In fact, the left-to-right direction of (4.26) also enjoys a purely string-diagrammatic argument, so let us draw some pictures. Using the data of an equivalence, we can form four different snakes – composites that are not necessarily identities:

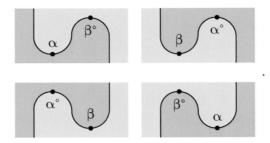

Why four? Because we can reflect a string diagram vertically, exchanging $\alpha \leftrightarrow \alpha°$ and $\beta \leftrightarrow \beta°$, and we can interchange the functors, exchanging $\alpha \leftrightarrow \beta$ and $\alpha° \leftrightarrow \beta°$. The latter move amounts to a color flip, exchanging yellow $\leftrightarrow$ orange.

The ability to reflect diagrams vertically gives rise to an easy-to-use proof principle:

$$\sigma = \tau \quad \Longleftrightarrow \quad \sigma° = \tau°, \tag{4.27}$$

cutting down the work by half. If we establish one equality, we get the dual equality between vertical reflections for free. Unfortunately, we cannot quarter the work: that equalities are preserved under color flips requires proof. Speculating a little bit, we would need a "color flipper,"

$$\includegraphics{} = \includegraphics{}, \tag{4.28}$$

a vertical sweep line that, when moved across the diagram, exchanges the colors. Perhaps surprisingly, such a color flipper exists under certain circumstances, which we will explore in due course in Section 4.7.3.

Let us return to the four snakes. While these are not necessarily identities, we can vertically compose a snake with its vertical reflection to obtain one. Diagrammatically speaking, we form a yellow or an orange "ear." These composites are special in that they contain each available natural transformation exactly once. Playing around with the half-circles, we find that there are actually a dozen shapes that share this property; see Figure 4.1 – this solves Exercise (2.14). We did not bother to label the natural transformations, as the colors uniquely identify them. In addition to the ear, we meet two old acquaintances, the doughnut and the hourglass of Section 4.7.1, and we get to know a new one, the "spiral." All of them share the fate of the

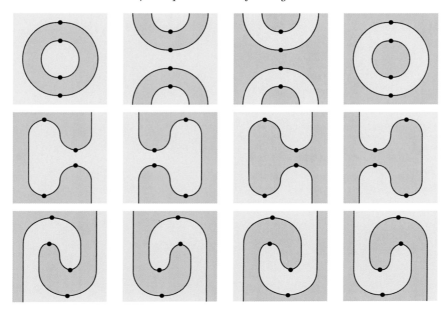

Figure 4.1 A dozen ways to combine α, β, α°, and β°.

ears in that they collapse to the identity. We have already conducted the proofs for the shapes in the first row, using two pops for the doughnuts and two snaps for the hourglasses. For the ears, we combine a snap with a pop (mostly for the effect – for the ear we combine a snake and its vertical reflection, so it is trivially the identity):

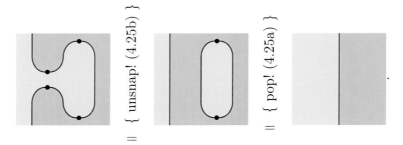

While these proofs are fairly straightforward, it is perhaps less clear how to squash a spiral – there is no obvious move, as the inverses do not directly face each other. However, observe that the spiral contains a snake in its center – it is almost an ear. The resemblance becomes more perspicuous if

we redraw the right ear slightly,

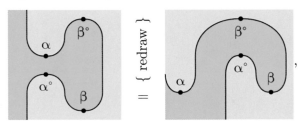

moving the upper cup to the left bottom of the diagram. This very cup is missing in the orange part of the spiral. Adding one by attaching a left ear allows us to squash a spiral. We see that the preceding move occurs twice during the calculation:

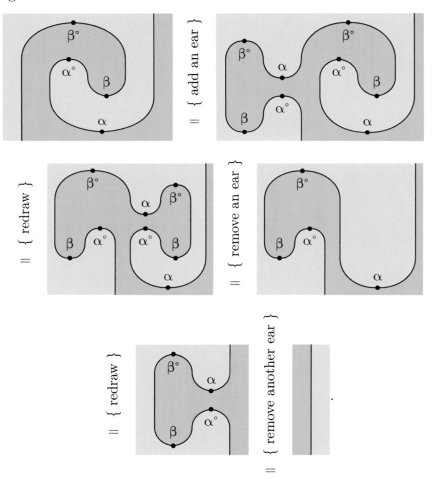

After these preliminary studies, we can now move on to constructing adjunctions. The recipe is as simple as it is appealing: we use one natural transformation for the counit (or unit) and compose the other three to form the unit (or counit). The snake equations are then automagically satisfied. Why? Because we have just demonstrated that all diagrams consisting of exactly four different natural transformation collapse to the identity! For example, we could pick α for the counit and compose the remaining three to obtain

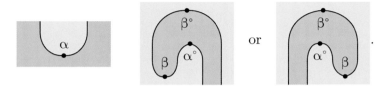

Recall that caps are bending devices: using α° and β°, we turn the arms of β into legs. The two candidates for the counit coincide, using a similar manoeuvre as in the preceding proof (see also Exercise 2.5). Now, if we form the snakes, combining the cup with one of the "hockey sticks," we obtain either an ear or a spiral (the only "single string" diagrams in Figure 4.1), which we can pull straight. So again, we obtain two unrelated adjunctions for F ⊣ G and two unrelated ones for G ⊣ F – the latter are, however, vertical reflections of the former.

Let us now assume that an equivalence of categories actually satisfies *one* of the snake equations. In this case, the other one holds as well, and we obtain a single adjoint equivalence for F ⊣ G and a single for G ⊣ F, one the vertical reflection of the other. That one snake equation implies the other can be seen as follows:

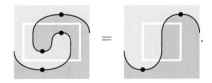

The cubicles on the left and on the right accommodate one snake equation. On both sides we have added a cap to the top and a cup to the bottom. We obtain the vertical reflection of the other snake equation on the right-hand side and a spiral on the left-hand side. Since the spiral can be straightened to a wire, the result follows.

4.7.3 Scan Lines, Snakes, and Hockey Sticks. We now return to the color flipper mentioned earlier, and how it relates to the snake equations. Throughout, we fix a pair of isomorphisms $\alpha : F \circ G \cong Id : \alpha°$ and $\beta : G \circ F \cong$

Id : β°. The ability to flip the color of a cup can be captured by the following equation:

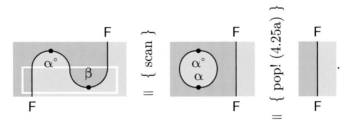

$$(4.29)$$

We will refer to this as a *scan equation*, as we scan the vertical line across the cup, flipping its color as we travel. Note that this is simply a more perspicuous rendering of the color changer (4.28).

Assuming the scan equation holds, we can prove a snake equation as follows:

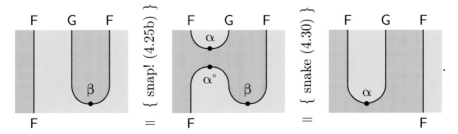

In the first step, we apply the scan equation to the lower half of the diagram.

If, on the other hand, we assume the snake equation

$$(4.30)$$

then we can prove the scan equation (4.29) as follows:

So the scan and snake equations are equally powerful.

We have seen the hockey stick diagram earlier. If we assume the preceding snake equation (4.30), then clearly the following equation, converting a hockey stick to a cup, holds:

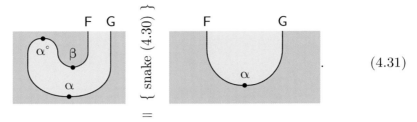

$$(4.31)$$

Recall, it does not matter which way the blade of our hockey stick faces, as the two possibilities are equal. The preceding *hockey stick equation* (4.31) identifies the counits of the two adjoint equivalences for F ⊣ G, so the two adjunctions "collapse" into one.

Conversely, if we instead assume the hockey stick equation (4.31), we can prove the snake equation (4.30) as follows:

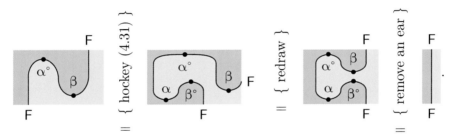

In the first step, we exploit our ability to vertically flip equations involving isomorphisms. This allows us to replace α° with the inverted hockey stick. We also deform the resulting picture to a familiar ear shape, in preparation for the final step.

Summarizing, we have seen that the snake, scan, and hockey stick equations are logically equivalent. As we saw previously, one snake equation implies the other, and so one scan or hockey stick equation is sufficient for the other to hold. Combined with our ability to vertically flip equations, any of these equations actually implies eleven more!

4.7.4 Fully Faithful and Essentially Surjective Functors. A functor that is part of an equivalence is fully faithful and essentially bijective. The converse also is true, assuming we do not worry about the notorious axiom of choice. In fact, since fully faithful implies essentially injective (1.20), the statement can be strengthened: the categories $\mathcal{C}$ and $\mathcal{D}$ are equivalent if and only if there is a functor F : $\mathcal{C} \to \mathcal{D}$ that is fully faithful and essentially surjective. Recall that the latter property means that for every $B : \mathcal{D}$ there is an $A : \mathcal{C}$ with $B \cong \mathsf{F}\,A$. The *axiom of choice* gives us an object map $\mathsf{G} : \mathcal{C} \leftarrow \mathcal{D}$ and a transformation α with $\alpha\,B : \mathsf{F}\,(\mathsf{G}\,B) \cong B$. We have to turn G into a functor, and we have to show that α is natural. We can actually derive the definition of G from the naturality condition. Let $f : A \to B$; then

$$f \cdot \alpha\,A = \alpha\,B \cdot \mathsf{F}\,(\mathsf{G}\,f)$$
$$\Longleftrightarrow \quad \{ \ \alpha\,B \text{ isomorphism } \}$$
$$(\alpha\,B)^{\circ} \cdot f \cdot \alpha\,A = \mathsf{F}\,(\mathsf{G}\,f)$$
$$\Longleftrightarrow \quad \{ \ \mathsf{F} \text{ fully faithful } \}$$
$$\mathsf{F}^{\circ}_{\mathsf{G}\,A, \mathsf{G}\,B}\,((\alpha\,B)^{\circ} \cdot f \cdot \alpha\,A) = \mathsf{G}\,f.$$

It is straightforward to show that G is functorial, as the "inverse" $\mathsf{F}^{\circ}_{\mathsf{G}\,A, \mathsf{G}\,B}$ (see Section 1.6.2) preserves identity and composition.

Summary

An adjunction consists of a pair of functors:

$$\mathcal{C} \; \underset{R}{\overset{L}{\rightleftarrows}} \; \mathcal{D} \; ,$$

and a pair of natural transformations:

Categories, adjunctions, and mates form the 2-category **Adj**.

Every adjunction $\mathsf{L} \dashv \mathsf{R}$ induces two adjunctions between functor categories: $\mathsf{L}\circ - \dashv \mathsf{R}\circ -$ and $-\circ\mathsf{R} \dashv -\circ\mathsf{L}$.

$$\mathsf{L}\circ A \mathrel{\dot{\to}} B \; \cong \; A \mathrel{\dot{\to}} \mathsf{R}\circ B \qquad \text{and} \qquad A\circ\mathsf{R} \mathrel{\dot{\to}} B \; \cong \; A \mathrel{\dot{\to}} B\circ\mathsf{L}$$

There are three different notions of "sameness" for categories, in decreasing order of strength: identity, isomorphism, and equivalence.

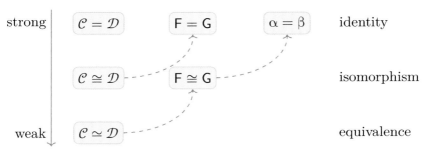

Isomorphism of categories relies on identity of functors; equivalence of categories relies on isomorphism of functors, which in turn relies on identity of natural transformations.

Let F be a functor. The following statements are equivalent: (a) F is part of an adjoint equivalence; (b) F is part of an equivalence; (c) F is fully faithful and essentially surjective.

In the previous chapter, we saw examples of Kleisli and Eilenberg–Moore categories that were isomorphic to familiar categories. Really, we should consider categories up to equivalence. With this broader perspective, we find new relationships. For example, **Par** is equivalent to **Set**^{Maybe}, but *not* isomorphic to it. Dually, **Set**$_\bullet$ is equivalent but not isomorphic to **Set**$_{\text{Maybe}}$.

Further Reading

Adjunctions are a central contribution of category theory. The concept was first isolated by Kan (1958).

Hinze (2013), Hinze et al. (2013), and Hinze and Wu (2016) show how to standardize a multitude of different recursion schemes using adjunctions, exemplifying their great unifying power. Category theory in general, and adjunctions in particular, enable us to build bridges between different parts of science. Gibbons et al. (2018), for example, use adjunctions to explain database query languages and query optimizations.

Exercises

4.1 ○ Summarize the contents of this chapter in your own words.

4.2 ○ Using equivalence (4.7), show that the image of the identity $L\,A \to L\,A$ under the bijection (4.1) is $\eta\,A$. Dually, show that the image of the identity $R\,B \to R\,B$ under the inverse bijection (4.1) is $\epsilon\,B$.

4.3 ⊙ Let P and Q be preorders. Show that $l : P \leftarrow Q$ and $r : P \to Q$ are monotone if

$$l\,a \leqslant b \iff a \leqslant r\,b \tag{4.32}$$

for all $a \in Q$ and $b \in \mathsf{P}$.

4.4 ◉ Show that the forgetful functor **Pre** → **Set** that forgets about the ordering has both a left and a right adjoint, and that these are different.

4.5 ◉ (a) The category **Inv** of involution algebras has as objects pairs $(A, f : A \to A)$ with $f \cdot f = id_A$, and as arrows $h : (A, f) \to (B, g)$ functions $h : A \to B$ with $h \cdot f = g \cdot h$. Show that the forgetful functor $\mathsf{U} : \mathbf{Inv} \to \mathbf{Set}$ has both a left and a right adjoint: $\mathsf{S} \dashv \mathsf{U} \dashv \mathsf{P}$, where

$$\mathsf{S}\, X = (X + X, inr \triangledown inl) \qquad \mathsf{P}\, X = (X \times X, outr \vartriangle outl).$$

$$\mathbf{Inv} \;\underset{\mathsf{U}}{\overset{\mathsf{S}}{\underset{\perp}{\rightleftarrows}}}\; \mathbf{Set} \;\underset{\mathsf{P}}{\overset{\mathsf{U}}{\underset{\perp}{\rightleftarrows}}}\; \mathbf{Inv}$$

(b) Repeat the exercise for idempotent algebras: $(A, f : A \to A)$ with $f \cdot f = f$. (c) Can you spot commonalities?

4.6 ⊙ Show that the following definition of adjunctions is equivalent to the one given in Section 4.1.

An adjunction can be specified by providing only part of the data. Surprisingly little is needed: Let $\mathsf{L} : \mathcal{C} \leftarrow \mathcal{D}$ be a functor, let $\mathsf{R} : \mathcal{C} \to \mathcal{D}$ be an object map, and let $\epsilon\, B : \mathsf{L}\,(\mathsf{R}\, B) \to B$ be a family of *universal arrows*. Universality means that, for each $f : \mathsf{L}\, A \to B : \mathcal{C}$, there exists a *unique* arrow $g : A \to \mathsf{R}\, B : \mathcal{D}$ such that $f = \epsilon\, B \cdot \mathsf{L}\, g$.

4.7 ◉ A category $\mathcal{C}$ is called *bicartesian closed* if the following adjunctions exist:

(1) *initial and terminal object*: $0 \dashv \Delta \dashv 1$ where $\Delta\, A = ()$;
(2) *coproducts and products*: $(+) \dashv \Delta \dashv (\times)$ where $\Delta\, A = (A, A)$;
(3) *exponentials*: $(- \times P) \dashv (-)^P$ for each object $P : \mathcal{C}$.

Assuming that $\mathcal{C}$ is bicartesian closed, (a) prove the so-called *laws of high-school algebra* (see Figure 4.2); (b) show that $\mathcal{C}$ is equivalent to the terminal category **1** if $\mathcal{C}$ has a zero object, $0 \cong 1$.

4.8 ⊙ Show that left adjoints preserve initial objects, $\mathsf{L}\, 0 \cong 0$, and right adjoints preserve terminal objects, $\mathsf{R}\, 1 \cong 1$.

4.9 ◉ An arrow $i : A \to A$ is called *idempotent* if $i \cdot i = i$; an idempotent is said to *split* if there exist arrows $f : A \to B$ and $g : B \to A$ such that $i = g \cdot f$ and $f \cdot g = id_B$. Given a pair of functors $\mathsf{K} : \mathcal{C} \leftarrow \mathcal{D}$ and

<table>
<tr><td colspan="2" align="center">sums</td><td colspan="2" align="center">products</td></tr>
</table>

sums	products
$X + 0 \cong X \cong 0 + X$	$X \times 1 \cong X \cong 1 \times X$
$X + Y \cong Y + X$	$X \times Y \cong Y \times X$
$(X + Y) + Z \cong X + (Y + Z)$	$(X \times Y) \times Z \cong X \times (Y \times Z)$

products and sums	exponentials and sums
$0 \times Z \cong 0$	$Z^0 \cong 1$
$(X + Y) \times Z \cong (X \times Z) + (Y \times Z)$	$Z^{X+Y} \cong Z^X \times Z^Y$

exponentials and products

$$1^X \cong 1$$
$$(Y \times Z)^X \cong Y^X \times Z^X$$
$$Z^1 \cong Z$$
$$Z^{X \times Y} \cong (Z^Y)^X$$

Figure 4.2 Laws of high-school algebra.

$\mathsf{R} : \mathcal{C} \to \mathcal{D}$ and a pair of natural transformations

and

such that

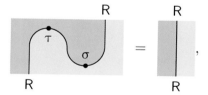

prove (a) that the composite

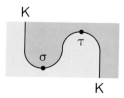

is an idempotent and (b) that R has a left adjoint if and only if this idempotent splits.

4.10 ● Let **Ring** be the category of rings and ring homomorphisms. The obvious forgetful functor **Ring** → **Set** has a left adjoint. Show that this adjunction can be obtained as a composite adjunction in two ways: **Ring** → **Ab** → **Set** and **Ring** → **Mon** → **Set**. Is it also possible to factor the free quantale construction in two different ways? See Exercise 4.6.

4.11 ○ Show that the mate of the identity is the identity and the mate of an iso is an iso.

4.12 ⊙ Show that the two "staircases" are related (4.20).

4.13 ● Show that for adjoint endofunctors $L \dashv R : C \rightharpoonup C$ and pairs of mates $\eta \dashv \epsilon$ and $\mu \dashv \delta$, the endofunctor L is a monad if and only if R is a comonad (4.21). Furthermore show that in this case, the Eilenberg–Moore category of L is isomorphic to the co-Eilenberg–Moore category of R (see Exercise 3.20). The curry adjunction provides an example where the left adjoint is a monad: the "write to a monoid" or writer monad; see Example 3.7. Its right adjoint $R = (-)^M$ is then a comonad, the "read from a monoid" comonad.

4.14 ⊙ Continuing Exercise 4.13, assume an adjoint situation $(L, \eta, \mu) \dashv (R, \epsilon, \delta)$, where a monad is left adjoint to a comonad. Using the units of the adjunction, we can bend the left arm and the leg of the multiplication so that

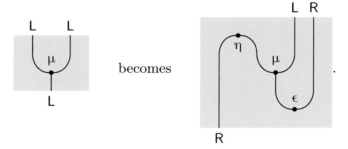

becomes

Show that the composite on the right is a left action of M.

4.15 ⊙ A preorder is a reflexive and transitive relation; a partial order is an antisymmetric preorder. Show that the category **Poset** of partial orders is a reflective subcategory of **Pre**.

4.16 ⊙ Given an adjunction $L \dashv R : C \rightharpoonup D$ with L full, show that $R \circ \epsilon$ and $\eta \circ R$ are inverses.

4.17 ⊙ The categories **Mon** and **Pre** are full subcategories of **Cat**. Are they reflective or coreflective?

4.18 ⊙ Give an example of an equivalence so that $\alpha : F{\circ}G \cong Id_{\mathcal{D}}$ and $\beta : Id_{\mathcal{C}} \cong G{\circ}F$ do not satisfy the snake equations.

4.19 ⊙ Confirm diagrammatically that if $L \dashv R$ with counit ϵ and unit η both isomorphisms, then $R \dashv L$ with counit η° and unit ϵ°. You may find the bubble-popping (4.25a) and double wire-snapping equations (4.25b) useful.

4.20 ⬤ A *Frobenius monad* is a monad (M, η, μ) with two additional gadgets:

The colollipop $\varepsilon : M \dashrightarrow Id$ allows you to "run" a monad, while the cap $\bar{\eta} : Id \dashrightarrow M{\circ}M$ enables you to bend wires downwards, turning arms into legs. The entities are subject to the following two coherence conditions:

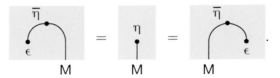

Bending ε to the right or to the left yields η.

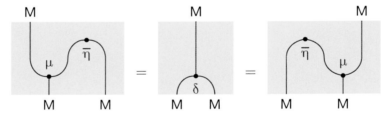

Bending the right arm of μ is the same as bending the left arm; either composite can be used to define $\delta : M \dashrightarrow M{\circ}M$.

(a) Show that (M, ε, δ) is a comonad.
(b) Use ε and μ to define $\bar{\varepsilon} : M{\circ}M \dashrightarrow Id$. Show that $\bar{\varepsilon} : M \dashv M : \bar{\eta}$.
(c) Show that $(M, \varepsilon, \delta) \dashv (M, \eta, \mu)$ and vice versa.
(d) Conclude that $\bar{\varepsilon} \dashv \bar{\eta}$, and vice versa.

4.21 ⊙ Continuing Exercise 4.20 show that the left-facing caterpillar is the same as the right-facing caterpillar:

4.22 ◉ Here is an alternative definition of Frobenius monads (see Exercise 4.20) that is nicely symmetric. An endofunctor M equipped with a comonad structure (M, ε, δ) and a monad structure (M, η, μ) is called Frobenius if the following *interaction axioms* are satisfied:

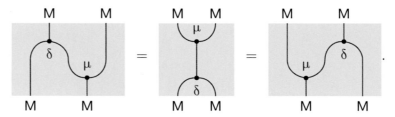

Show that the two definitions of Frobenius are equivalent.

5

Putting It All Together

Our hope is that by this point, we have developed some dexterity in manipulating string diagrams. Chapters 3 and 4 also introduced the diagrammatic basics of monads and adjunctions.

With these tools in place, it is time to put our skills to the test. This chapter combines many of the ideas we have encountered in order to investigate some more elaborate examples involving universal constructions, and various combinations of monads and adjunctions. The examples also provide the opportunity to introduce a few more diagrammatic tricks, such as imploding and exploding composite natural transformations as a form of abstraction, and a box notation for reasoning about universal constructions.

5.1 Huber's Construction

Calculations using string diagrams, like conventional symbolic calculations, mainly involve replacing equals by equals, applying what is known as Leibniz's law. An important special case concerns the use of definitions, where a definiens is replaced by a definiendum or vice versa, expanding or collapsing an expression. While entirely straightforward in symbolic manipulations, it is sometimes a source of confusion in diagrammatic moves, in particular, as it often involves the "explosion" or "implosion" of vertices and edges. We illustrate this with an important result.

Monads and adjunctions are intimately related. Huber (1961) showed that a monad $M : \mathcal{C} \to \mathcal{C}$ and an adjunction $L \dashv R : \mathcal{C} \rightharpoonup \mathcal{D}$ yield a monad $T := R \circ M \circ L : \mathcal{D} \to \mathcal{D}$:

$$M \circlearrowleft \mathcal{C} \underset{R}{\overset{L}{\underset{\perp}{\rightleftarrows}}} \mathcal{D} \ .$$

To construct unit and multiplication of the composite monad T we "outline" the given operations of M:

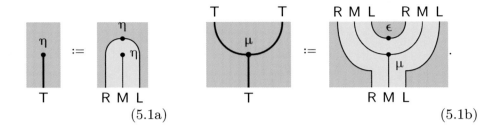

$$(5.1a) \qquad\qquad\qquad\qquad\qquad\qquad (5.1b)$$

We refer to this technique as *Huber's construction*. Diagrammatically, we put a cap on M's lollipop and border M's fork with R and L, additionally placing a cup between the prongs of the fork. The diagrams on the left are defined by the diagrams on the right. We draw "fat wires" for the edges corresponding to the functor T to emphasize that it is a composite.

When the definitions of these composites are used in a calculation, the vertices and edges are "exploded" to reveal the internal structure or "imploded" to conceal the structure. In particular, the diagrams on the right-hand side feature an internal region, which is contracted on the left-hand side – conversely, the monochromatic diagrams for monads become dichromatic in adjunction land. You may wish to think of T as a "superedge" and of $\eta : \mathsf{Id} \xrightarrow{.} \mathsf{T}$ and $\mu : \mathsf{T} \circ \mathsf{T} \xrightarrow{.} \mathsf{T}$ as "supernodes" (perhaps as in UML state diagrams).

We check the first monad unit axiom (3.2a) as follows:

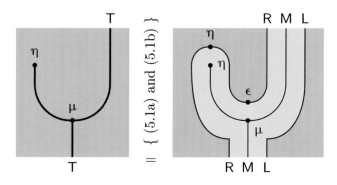

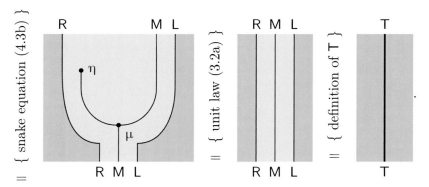

The other unit axiom is established using an analogous calculation. The proof of the associativity axiom (3.2b) only relies on the corresponding law for the underlying monad M.

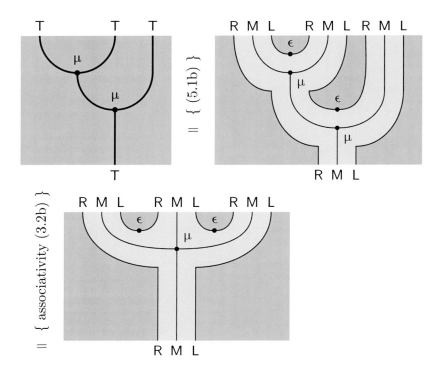

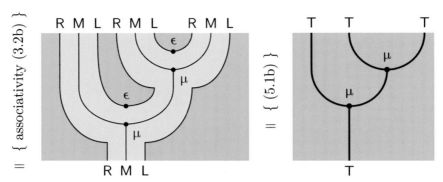

After the second step we have added the three-pronged fork of the composite for clarity. In general, the n-pronged fork for T is given by the "outline" of the n-pronged fork for M with $n-1$ cups placed between each pair of adjacent prongs.

A special case of Huber's construction is worth singling out: instantiating the underlying monad to the identity, we have that an adjunction $\mathsf{L} \dashv \mathsf{R}$ induces a monad $(\mathsf{R} \circ \mathsf{L}, \eta, \mathsf{R} \circ \epsilon \circ \mathsf{L})$. The unit of the adjunction serves as the unit of the composite monad; its multiplication is given by the composite $\mathsf{R} \circ \epsilon \circ \mathsf{L}$.

Moreover, by reflecting the diagrams vertically, we obtain the dual of Huber's construction: a comonad $\mathsf{N} : \mathcal{D} \to \mathcal{D}$ and an adjunction $\mathsf{L} \dashv \mathsf{R} : \mathcal{C} \to \mathcal{D}$ yield a comonad $\mathsf{L} \circ \mathsf{N} \circ \mathsf{R} : \mathcal{C} \to \mathcal{C}$. In particular, we have that an adjunction $\mathsf{L} \dashv \mathsf{R}$ induces a comonad $(\mathsf{L} \circ \mathsf{R}, \epsilon, \mathsf{L} \circ \eta \circ \mathsf{R})$.

5.1.1 Examples of Huber's Construction. Several examples of monads and comonads we have encountered before can be reinterpreted using Huber's construction.

Example 5.1 (Pointed Sets). The *category of pointed sets*, **Set**$_\bullet$ has as objects sets with a special designated element, written $\bot$, and as arrows functions that preserve these special elements, $f \bot_A = \bot_B$. There is an obvious forgetful functor $\mathsf{U} : \mathbf{Set}_\bullet \to \mathbf{Set}$. This functor has a left adjoint $\mathsf{F} : \mathbf{Set} \to \mathbf{Set}_\bullet$, adding a new element to each set, and extending each function so that it preserves it.

$$\mathbf{Set}_\bullet \underset{\mathsf{U}}{\overset{\mathsf{F}}{\underset{\longrightarrow}{\overset{\longleftarrow}{\bot}}}} \mathbf{Set}$$

Using Huber's construction, we can recover the maybe monad of Example 3.5 as $\mathsf{Maybe} = \mathsf{U} \circ \mathsf{F}$. □

Example 5.2 (State Monad and Costate Comonad). Turning to an application of the full result, we observe that the state monad is induced by the curry adjunction: $\mathsf{State}_P = (-)^P \circ (- \times P)$. Moreover, we can add state to an arbitrary monad, $(-)^P \circ \mathsf{M} \circ (- \times P)$, obtaining the so-called *state monad transformer*.

Dually, the costate comonad is obtained by composing the adjuncts in reverse order: $\mathsf{CoState}_P = (- \times P) \circ (-)^P$. Inserting a comonad in the middle, $(- \times P) \circ \mathsf{N} \circ (-)^P$, yields the *costate comonad transformer*. □

Example 5.3 (State Transformers). Now that we know more about the structure of the state monad, it is a good time to relate the state monad to a more ad hoc way of dealing with state in functional programming:

$$A \times P \to B \times P \quad \text{versus} \quad A \to \mathsf{State}\, B.$$

A simple technique is to pass in the state as an additional argument and to return the updated state as an additional result. The curry adjunction implies that the two types of programs are in one-to-one correspondence:

$$\mathsf{L}\, A \to \mathsf{L}\, B \;\cong\; A \to \mathsf{R}\, (\mathsf{L}\, B). \tag{5.2}$$

Diagrammatically, an arm is turned into a leg:

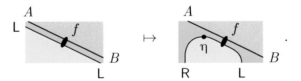

We draw our state transformers as slightly oval "blobs." This allows the input and output pairs of wires to be drawn in parallel, avoiding any distracting kinks in our diagrams. This is a common technique when using string diagrams. Vertices can be depicted as dots, boxes, ovals, or other shapes that permit the convenient connection of their input and output wires. We will see some even bigger "blobs" in ESD Chapter 4.

The correspondence (5.2) preserves identity and composition. The identity state transformer is related to the unit of the state monad:

The composition of two state transformers is related to the Kleisli composition of the corresponding stateful computations:

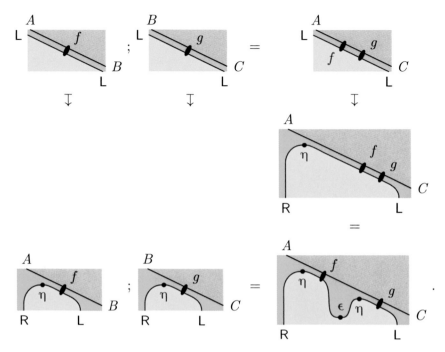

Observe that the Kleisli composition in the composite monad $R \circ L$ simply connects the L wire of the first arrow to the R wire of the second arrow via a cup.

As a final remark, when inspecting the proofs we observe that they are not specific to state; rather, they hold for an arbitrary adjunction and its induced monad. We get back to this point in ESD Chapter 3. □

As promised at the end of Section 4.5, we now see that given suitable adjoints, Huber's construction yields a source of adjoint monads and comonads.

Example 5.4 (Adjoint Triples). Assume that we have three functors forming an *adjoint triple* or a *string of adjunctions*:

$$L \dashv M \dashv R,$$

so that M is (and has) both a left and a right adjoint. We saw in Section 4.3 that we can compose adjunctions, yielding:

$$M \circ L \dashv M \circ R \qquad \text{and} \qquad L \circ M \dashv R \circ M.$$

Huber's construction tells us that $R \circ M$ is a monad with *left* adjoint comonad $L \circ M$, and $M \circ L$ is a monad with a *right* adjoint comonad $M \circ R$.

Of course, what remains now is to find a source of adjoint triples. We will find such a source in ESD Chapter 6. □

5.1.2 Upgrading Arrows. In some sense, Huber's construction combines two monads: the given monad M and the monad R∘L. Whenever we combine monads, it is desirable to also provide maps that upgrade the component monads into the composite.

Here, we will consider upgrading the monad R∘L to the monad R∘M∘L. We relegate upgrading M to ESD Chapter 5. The latter task is less straightforward, as M and R∘M∘L possibly live in different categories.

For example, if we apply Huber's construction to the curry adjunction $(-) \times X \dashv (-)^X$ and the list monad, we hope to upgrade a stateful computation $(- \times X)^X$ to a "multi-output," stateful computation $(\mathsf{List}\,(- \times X))^X$ producing a list of outputs and subsequent states. It is useful to generalize the task slightly: given a monad map $\tau : \mathsf{S} \dashrightarrow \mathsf{T}$, we show that

is a monad map, as well. For the proofs we apply the axioms for the underlying monad map. For the unit axiom:

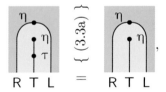

and for the multiplication axiom:

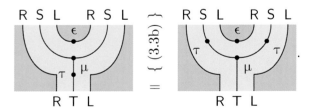

Note that the adjoint functors and their units are completely passive.

Since the unit $\eta : \mathsf{Id} \dashrightarrow \mathsf{M}$ is a monad map, the original task falls out as a special case: $\mathsf{R}\circ\eta\circ\mathsf{L} : \mathsf{R}\circ\mathsf{L} \dashrightarrow \mathsf{R}\circ\mathsf{M}\circ\mathsf{L}$. For our concrete example, applying the state monad transformer to the list monad, the resulting monad map

$$(- \times P) \circ \eta \circ (-)^P : (- \times P)^P \dot{\to} (\mathsf{List}\,(- \times P))^P$$

sends a stateful computation to the corresponding computation, producing a single element list of outputs.

5.2 Universal Constructions

We have noted on several occasions that the concept of an adjunction enjoys several complementary definitions. The ones we have used in Chapter 4 describe a perfectly symmetric situation: and the left and the right adjoint, the counit and the unit, the left and the right transposition are treated on an equal footing. However, the different examples of adjunctions that we have encountered paint quite a different picture. Typically, one adjoint functor is simple, or even trivial such as the diagonal functor or a forgetful functor. However, via the adjunction it gives rise to an interesting, or even rich, concept such as a product or a free construction.

An asymmetric perspective is actually most useful when an adjoint situation has to be established as it simply means less work. Since the components of an adjunction are interdefinable, an adjunction can be specified by providing only part of the data. Surprisingly little is actually needed: a functor, an object map, and a so-called universal transformation, a concept that we explore in two steps.

In this section, we deal with some awkward customers; for example maps we do not know are functorial, and transformations that we need to establish are natural. The diagrammatic approach is effective in such situations as well, as we shall demonstrate. We also have not seen much of the traditional symbolic notation for a while, so we also provide some symbolic computations in what follows for contrast with the diagrammatic calculations.

5.2.1 Universal Arrows. Definitions in category theory often take the form of universal constructions. The paradigmatic example of this approach is the definition of products, which we have encountered in Section 1.3.2 – in fact, this is also historically the first example. The general concept is as follows.

Given a functor $\mathsf{R} : \mathcal{C} \to \mathcal{D}$ and an object $A : \mathcal{D}$, a *universal arrow from A to* R consists of an object $L_A : \mathcal{C}$ and an arrow $\eta_A : A \to \mathsf{R}\,L_A : \mathcal{D}$, which we prefer to draw in a curvy style:

The data has to satisfy the so-called *universal property*: for each object $B :$ $\mathcal{C}$ and for each arrow $g : A \to \mathsf{R}\,B : \mathcal{D}$, there exists a *unique* arrow $f : L_A \to$ $B : \mathcal{C}$ such that $\mathsf{R}f \cdot \eta_A = g$. The unique arrow is sometimes called the *mediating arrow*. The universal property can be stated more attractively if we replace the existentially quantified variable f by a Skolem function[1], cunningly written like a transposition $\lceil - \rceil$. Using this gadget, the statement reads: for each object $B : \mathcal{C}$ and for each arrow $g : A \to \mathsf{R}\,B : \mathcal{D}$, there exists an arrow $\lceil g \rceil : L_A \to B : \mathcal{C}$ such that

$$f = \lceil g \rceil \quad \Longleftrightarrow \quad \mathsf{R}f \cdot \eta_A = g, \tag{5.3}$$

for all $f : L_A \to B : \mathcal{C}$. The equivalence captures the existence of an arrow f satisfying the property on the right and furthermore states that $\lceil g \rceil$ is the unique such arrow. Observe the asymmetry: the object A is fixed in advance, whereas the object B is universally quantified.

The transposition maps an arrow in $\mathcal{D}$ to an arrow in $\mathcal{C}$. In our graphical calculus it is integrated as a *box*.

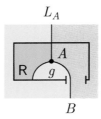

The arrow g features three edges, only two of which cross the border: the R-edge is a cul-de-sac. The two borders are quite different in nature. The border station on the lower boundary is "open," indicated visually by a hole; the B edge is allowed to cross without further ado. By contrast, the border station on the upper boundary is "closed"; whilst passing the station, the L_A edge transmogrifies into an A edge. We shall see that the border type has

---

[1] The existentially quantified variable f is in the scope of a universal quantifier, hence the need for a Skolem *function*.

an impact on admissible movements. The colors visualize that the arrow g lives in $\mathcal{D}$, whereas its transpose $\lceil g \rceil$ lives in $\mathcal{C}$. Across the open border, the yellow and gray colors flow into the box.

The asymmetry of the universal property (5.3) is reflected in its diagrammatic representation, which governs the interplay of bending and boxing:

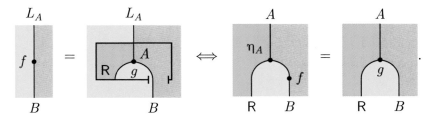

Like the unit of an adjunction, a universal can be seen as a bending device, turning an L_A arm into an R leg and an A arm. However, contrast the equivalence to (4.7) which captures a perfectly symmetric, adjoint situation.

The universal property (5.3) has three immediate consequences that are worth singling out. If we make the left-hand side true by instantiating f to $\lceil g \rceil$, we obtain the *computation or cancellation law*:

$$\mathsf{R} \lceil g \rceil \cdot \eta_A = g. \tag{5.4a}$$

Diagrammatically, bending is a pre-inverse of boxing:

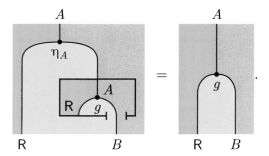

The equality is called the computation law as it is sometimes used as a left-to-right rewrite rule in a computational setting.

Conversely, setting f to the identity id_{L_A}, we can make the right-hand side of (5.3) true, if we instantiate g to η_A. This instance of the universal property is known as the *reflection or identity law*:

$$id_{L_A} = \lceil \eta_A \rceil. \tag{5.4b}$$

Boxing the bender gives the identity; the L_A values travel to the other side only to be reflected back:

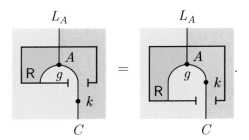

Finally, the *fusion law* allows us to fuse a transpose with an arrow to form another transpose:

$$k \cdot \lceil g \rceil = \lceil \mathsf{R}\, k \cdot g \rceil, \tag{5.4c}$$

for all $k : B' \to B''$. The law states that the transpose $\lceil - \rceil$ is natural in the target type B. The diagrammatic rendering of fusion is instructive:

The arrow k is allowed to freely cross the open border. In diagrammatic proofs, we may decide to omit explicit invocations of (5.4c). Unsurprisingly, free movement is not possible on the upper boundary.

For the proof of fusion we appeal to the universal property:

$$k \cdot \lceil g \rceil = \lceil \mathsf{R}\, k \cdot g \rceil \quad \Longleftrightarrow \quad \mathsf{R}\, (k \cdot \lceil g \rceil) \cdot \eta_A = \mathsf{R}\, k \cdot g.$$

To show the right-hand side, we calculate

$$
\begin{aligned}
& \mathsf{R}\, (k \cdot \lceil g \rceil) \cdot \eta_A \\
={} & \{\ \mathsf{R} \text{ functor (1.11b) }\} \\
& \mathsf{R}\, k \cdot \mathsf{R}\, \lceil g \rceil \cdot \eta_A \\
={} & \{\ \text{computation law (5.4a) }\} \\
& \mathsf{R}\, k \cdot g.
\end{aligned}
$$

As the functor law is integrated into our graphical calculus, the diagrammatic proof only appeals to the computation law:

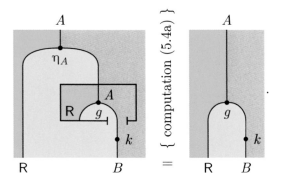

Conversely, computation, reflection, and fusion imply the universal property. The left-to-right direction of (5.3) amounts to the computation law (5.4a). For the right-to-left direction, we combine fusion and reflection:

$$\lceil Rf \cdot \eta_A \rceil$$
$$= \quad \{ \text{ fusion law (5.4c) } \}$$
$$f \cdot \lceil \eta_A \rceil$$
$$= \quad \{ \text{ reflection law (5.4b) } \}$$
$$f.$$

The pictorial proof is left as an instructive exercise to the reader.

5.2.2 Universal Transformations. Let us now assume that a universal arrow exists for *every* object $A : \mathcal{D}$. This family of universals gives rise to a family of objects, that is, an object map $L : \mathcal{C} \leftarrow \mathcal{D}$, and a family of arrows, that is, a transformation $\eta\, A : A \to R\,(L\,A)$. Of course, we would like L and η to be proper categorical gadgets. It turns out that there is a *unique* way to turn the object map L into a functor so that the transformation η is natural in A:

$$R\,(L\,h) \cdot \eta\,A = \eta\,B \cdot h,$$

for all arrows $h : A \to B$. The diagrammatic notation is again instructive:

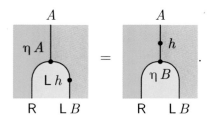

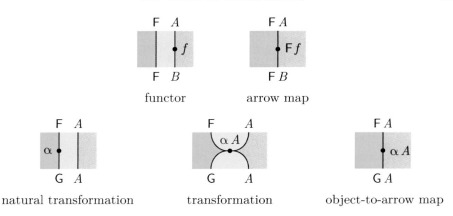

natural transformation   transformation   object-to-arrow map

Figure 5.1 Diagrammatic rendering of good and awkward customers.

Naturality means that we can move an $\mathsf{L}\,h$ arrow upwards, turning it into an h arrow. Inspecting the diagram, it may seem that we are violating our own principles by mixing diagrammatic and symbolic notation. The use of symbolic notation is, however, unavoidable: we do not yet know whether L is functorial and whether η is natural, consequently we cannot assume this in our graphical calculations. In particular, we are not allowed to draw L as a separate edge. Figure 5.1 summarizes the different types of gadgets; see also Section 2.2.4.

To derive the functorial action of L on arrows, we appeal once again to the universal property:

$$\mathsf{L}\,h = \lceil \eta\,B \cdot h \rceil \quad \Longleftrightarrow \quad \mathsf{R}\,(\mathsf{L}\,h) \cdot \eta\,A = \eta\,B \cdot h,$$

which suggests we define

$$\mathsf{L}\,h := \lceil \eta\,B \cdot h \rceil. \tag{5.5a}$$

Reassuringly, we obtain a formula that we have encountered before (4.4c). Diagrammatically, we precompose h with the bender, boxing the result:

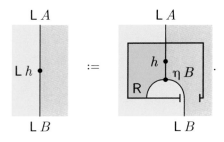

Section 4.6 provides a different graphical rendering (4.22) of this definition based on a snake equation. However, as boxing is the diagrammatic
counterpart of transposition, the preceding diagram is actually closer to the
symbolic version.

We postpone the proof that L preserves identity and composition and
first turn to naturality. The *functor fusion law* states that we can fuse the
composition of a transpose with an arrow of the form Lh to form another
transpose:

$$\lceil g \rceil \cdot \mathsf{L}\, h = \lceil g \cdot h \rceil, \tag{5.5b}$$

for all $h : {}'A \to A'$. The law formalizes that the transpose $\lceil - \rceil$ is also natural
in the source type A:

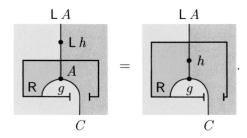

The closed border has become permeable. However, not any old arrow is
allowed to move from the outside to the inside: the arrow has to be of the
form Lh, which is then turned into an h arrow.

The proof of (5.5b) builds on fusion and computation:

$$
\begin{aligned}
&\quad \lceil g \rceil \cdot \mathsf{L}\, h \\
&= \quad \{ \text{ definition of L (5.5a) } \} \\
&\quad \lceil g \rceil \cdot \lceil \eta\, A' \cdot h \rceil \\
&= \quad \{ \text{ fusion law (5.4c) } \} \\
&\quad \lceil \mathsf{R}\lceil g \rceil \cdot \eta\, A' \cdot h \rceil \\
&= \quad \{ \text{ computation law (5.4a) } \} \\
&\quad \lceil g \cdot h \rceil.
\end{aligned}
$$

The description of functor fusion suggests that the arrow Lh is moved inside
the box. Inspecting the proof, we observe that the reality is quite different:
two boxes are chained together; using fusion, the lower box is actually moved

into the upper one! Laws can be deceiving:

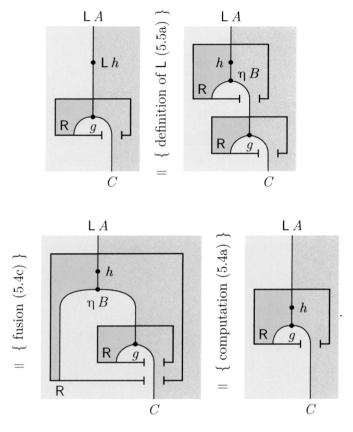

Given these prerequisites, it is straightforward to show that our aspiring functor L preserves identity,

$$L \, id_A$$

$= \quad \{ \text{ definition of L (5.5a) } \}$

$$\lceil \eta \, A \cdot id_A \rceil$$

$= \quad \{ \text{ identity (1.1a) } \}$

$$\lceil \eta \, A \rceil$$

$= \quad \{ \text{ reflection law (5.4b) } \}$

$$id_{L \, A},$$

and composition,

$$L \, g \cdot L \, f$$

$$= \quad \{ \text{ definition of } \mathsf{L} \text{ (5.5a) } \}$$
$$\lceil \eta \, C \cdot g \rceil \cdot \mathsf{L} f$$
$$= \quad \{ \text{ functor fusion (5.5b) } \}$$
$$\lceil \eta \, C \cdot g \cdot f \rceil$$
$$= \quad \{ \text{ definition of } \mathsf{L} \text{ (5.5a) } \}$$
$$\mathsf{L} \, (g \cdot f).$$

The second functor law is simply an instance of functor fusion.

The corresponding diagrammatic arguments are short and elegant, and the explicit type information makes it easier to see the manipulations going on:

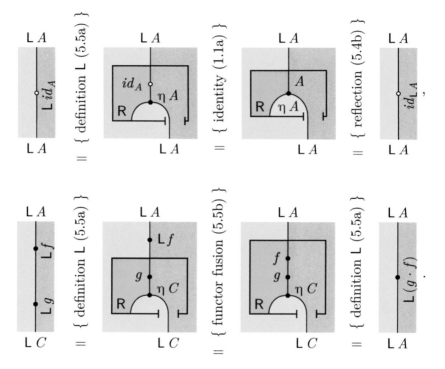

Everything is restored to good health now. We are back to a perfectly symmetric, adjoint situation: there are functors L and R, natural transformations ϵ and η with $\epsilon \, B = \lceil id_{\mathsf{R} \, B} \rceil$, and left and right transpositions with $\lfloor f \rfloor = \mathsf{R} f \cdot \eta \, A$. The fusion properties (5.4c) and (5.5b) furthermore imply that the transpositions are natural in both A and B (4.2b). (As an aside, we have essentially solved Exercise 4.6, which deals with the dual situation, where a functor $\mathsf{L} : \mathcal{C} \leftarrow \mathcal{D}$, an object map $\mathsf{R} : \mathcal{C} \to \mathcal{D}$, and a *universal transformation* $\epsilon \, B : \mathsf{L} \, (\mathsf{R} \, B) \to B$ are given.)

5.2.3 Boxing. If we wish, we can continue to use boxing in our graphical calculations; in fact, for both left and right transpositions. However, we should redraw the boxes to account for the fact that both L and R are functorial:

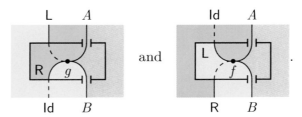

The single L A edge has been split into two here. For emphasis we have also added identity edges. In a sense, L transmogrifies into Id when entering the box, and R transmogrifies into Id when leaving the box.

As usual, the properties of an adjunction translate into graphical movements: the bijection of arrows (4.1) means that two nested boxes of opposite types cancel each other out; the naturality of the bijection (4.2a) and (4.2b) allows us to freely slide arrows on the A and B wires across the boundaries. Visually, free movement is indicated by cutting holes into the box. The reader is invited to work out the details; see Exercise 5.11.

In the same way that the entities of an adjunction are interdefinable, in particular, the units and transpositions, the graphical gadgets are interdefinable:

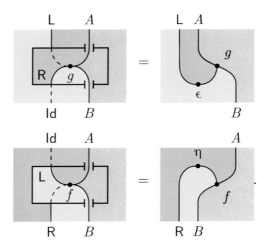

The equations are the diagrammatic counterparts of (4.4a) and (4.4d).

Choosing which gadgets and which techniques to use is ultimately a matter of good taste. Bending works well for proofs that involve mainly natural transformations, in particular, as naturality is built into the notation. Boxing is often the technique of choice if mainly objects and arrows are involved. The proofs are, however, more pedestrian, as naturality has to be invoked explicitly. Whatever your preferred choice, keep in mind that *boxing is bending.*

5.3 Free Monads

We saw free monoids in Example 1.22. If we think of monoids as sets with extra structure, intuitively free monoids are the "simplest possible way" of building a monoid from a given set.

By analogy, we can think of monads as *functors* with extra structure. It is then natural to ask if there is a canonical way of building a monad from a given functor, that is, can we build free monads? This is the question we shall now investigate.

5.3.1 Free Algebras. In Section 3.5.1 we introduced the category of algebras for an endofunctor Σ, which equips a given category $\mathcal{C}$ with additional structure. There is a forgetful functor, the *underlying functor*,

$$\mathsf{U}^\Sigma : \Sigma\text{-}\mathbf{Alg}(\mathcal{C}) \to \mathcal{C} \qquad \begin{aligned} \mathsf{U}^\Sigma(A, a) &:= A, \\ \mathsf{U}^\Sigma(h) &:= h, \end{aligned} \qquad (5.6)$$

that forgets about this additional structure, mapping an algebra to its carrier and a homomorphism to its underlying arrow. The left adjoint to the forgetful functor sends an object to the *free algebra* or *term algebra*:

$$\Sigma\text{-}\mathbf{Alg}(\mathcal{C}) \underset{\mathsf{U}^\Sigma}{\overset{\mathsf{Free}^\Sigma}{\underset{\perp}{\rightleftarrows}}} \mathcal{C} \qquad \begin{aligned} \mathsf{Free}^\Sigma A &=: (\Sigma^* A, \mathsf{in}\, A) \\ \mathsf{Free}^\Sigma f &=: \Sigma^* f \end{aligned} \qquad (5.7)$$

If Σ is a polynomial functor on **Set**, then the left adjoint exists. The elements of the free algebra $\Sigma^* A$ are first-order terms built from symbols determined by Σ and variables drawn from A. Think of the functor Σ as a signature or a grammar describing the syntax of a language. The functorial action on arrows, the Σ-homomorphism $\Sigma^* f$, implements "renaming" of variables. The unit of the adjunction, $\mathsf{var}\, A : A \to \Sigma^* A$, turns a variable into a term. The action of the algebra in $A : \Sigma(\Sigma^* A) \to \Sigma^* A$ constructs a composite term from a Σ-structure of subterms. Finally, the counit $\epsilon(A, a) : \mathsf{Free}^\Sigma A \to (A, a)$ evaluates a term using the operations of a given algebra.

For the subsequent developments, it will be convenient to introduce a shorthand for the evaluation map: $\mathsf{U}^\Sigma(\epsilon(A, a))$. This is an arrow in the underlying category, which we shall denote $(\![a]\!)$, and pronounce "*fold a.*" Given an interpretation of symbols, an algebra a, the fold $(\![a]\!)$ interprets a term:

$$\frac{a : \Sigma\, A \to A}{(\![a]\!) : \Sigma^*\, A \to A}.$$

In diagrams, the fold $(\![a]\!)$ is depicted by a double circle, annotated with the target algebra a, see the left-side diagram in the following:

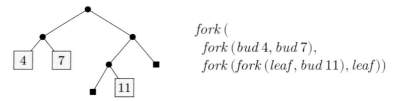

$$\tag{5.8}$$

Occasionally, an alternative drawing style using a rounded box is useful; see the diagram on the right. There, the algebra is drawn as a separate diagram within the box. This style is preferable if the algebra has structure, as it avoids the need to mix symbols and diagrams.

Example 5.5 (Binary Trees). Continuing Example 3.22, binary trees are elements of the free algebra of the functor $\Sigma\, A = 1 + A \times A$. They are formed using the data constructors *leaf*, *bud*, and *fork*, defined as follows

$$leaf : \Sigma^*\, X \qquad\qquad\qquad leaf = \mathsf{in}\, X\, (inl\,()),$$
$$bud : X \to \Sigma^*\, X \qquad\qquad\qquad bud\, x = \mathsf{var}\, X\, x,$$
$$fork : \Sigma^*\, X \times \Sigma^*\, X \to \Sigma^*\, X \qquad fork\, (l, r) = \mathsf{in}\, X\, (inr\, (l, r)),$$

where X is some set of variables, used for labeling the binary trees.

$$fork\,($$
$$\quad fork\,(bud\,4,\, bud\,7),$$
$$\quad fork\,(fork\,(leaf,\, bud\,11),\, leaf))$$

The fold $(\![sum]\!) : \Sigma^*\, \mathbb{N} \to \mathbb{N}$ with $sum : \Sigma\, \mathbb{N} \to \mathbb{N}$ defined as

$$sum\,(inl\,()) = 0$$
$$sum\,(inr\,(a, b)) = a + b$$

adds the elements of a tree, yielding $(4 + 7) + ((0 + 11) + 0) = 22$, for the preceding example tree. □

Remark 5.6 (Initial and Free Algebras). Example 3.22 touched upon initial algebras. The elements of an initial algebra can be seen as closed first-order terms, terms without variables. Free algebras generalize initial algebras, adding variables to the scene. Categorically speaking, as left adjoints preserve initial objects, $\mathsf{Free}^\Sigma\, 0$ is then the initial algebra. In **Set**, the initial object amounts to the empty set: terms whose variables are drawn from the empty set are closed terms. □

The adjunction $\mathsf{Free}^\Sigma \dashv \mathsf{U}^\Sigma$ captures that the meaning of a term is uniquely determined by the meaning of its variables. Expressed in terms of the underlying category, the universal property reads as follows:

$$\vcenter{\hbox{$\Sigma^* A \atop B$}} \;=\; \vcenter{\hbox{$\Sigma^*\quad A \atop B$}} \quad\Longleftrightarrow\quad \vcenter{\hbox{$A \atop B$}} \;=\; \vcenter{\hbox{$A \atop B$}} , \tag{5.9}$$

for all Σ-*homomorphisms* $h : \mathsf{Free}^\Sigma\, A \to (B, b)$ and all arrows $g : A \to B$. The homomorphism condition for arrows *from* the free algebra has an interesting graphical representation:

$$\vcenter{\hbox{$\Sigma\quad\Sigma^* A \atop B$}} \;=\; \vcenter{\hbox{$\Sigma\quad\Sigma^* A \atop B$}} .$$

Observe that the action of the free algebra is a natural transformation as the free functor yields Σ-homomorphisms – the naturality property of in coincides with the homomorphism condition for $\Sigma^* f$. We decided to draw the action of the free algebra as a tuning fork, so that the shape of the resulting equation resembles the multiplication axiom of Eilenberg–Moore algebras (3.8b).

It is instructive to consider some further consequences of the adjoint situation. First of all, we obtain the following *computation rules*:

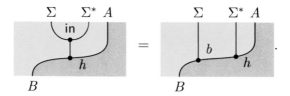

$$\tag{5.10a}$$

$$(5.10b)$$

The first computation rule, which is actually the second snake equation (4.3b) in disguise, formalizes that folding a variable simply yields its value ("does nothing"). The second computation rule captures that a fold itself is a Σ-homomorphism, $(\!(a)\!) : \mathsf{Free}^{\Sigma} A \to (A, a)$. This entails that the meaning function is compositional: the meaning of a composite term is defined in terms of the meanings of its constituent parts; evaluating a compound term proceeds by recursively evaluating the components and then applying the algebra to the result. Furthermore, the naturality of the counit gives rise to the *elevation rule*:

$$(5.10c)$$

Example 5.7. To illustrate the use of elevation, consider the function *double* $a = 2 \cdot a$. Since *double* $\cdot$ *sum* $=$ *sum* $\cdot \Sigma$ *double*[2], elevation implies

$$double \cdot (\!(sum)\!) = (\!(sum)\!) \cdot \Sigma^* \, double.$$

It does not matter whether we first sum the original tree and then double the result, or double the elements of a binary tree and then sum the resulting tree. The elevation rule is at the heart of an algebraic approach to program optimization. ☐

5.3.2 Relating Σ-Algebras and Algebras for a Monad. If we apply Huber's construction to the adjunction $\mathsf{Free}^{\Sigma} \dashv \mathsf{U}^{\Sigma}$, we obtain the so-called *free monad of a functor*: $(\Sigma^*, \mathsf{var}, \mathsf{sub})$ where $\mathsf{sub} = (\!(\mathsf{in})\!)$. Recall that the unit, $\mathsf{var}\, A : A \to \Sigma^* A$, turns a variable into a term. The multiplication $\mathsf{sub}\, A : \Sigma^* (\Sigma^* A) \to \Sigma^* A$ corresponds to substitution, flattening a term whose variables are again terms. Substitution plays nicely with evaluation.

---

[2] Do not confuse the signature functor Σ with the symbol $\sum$ for summation.

Combining (5.10b) and (5.10c) gives

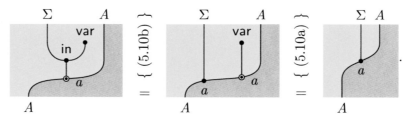

$$(5.10d)$$

which records that the two ways of evaluating a nested term of type $\Sigma^* (\Sigma^* A)$ are equivalent.

The Eilenberg–Moore category of the free monad has as objects algebras of type $\Sigma^* A \to A$. Given a Σ-algebra (A, a), we can form a Σ^*-algebra using fold: $(A, (\!(a)\!))$. It turns out that every Eilenberg–Moore algebra arises this way. Categorically speaking, the category of Σ-algebras is isomorphic to the Eilenberg–Moore category of the free monad Σ^*:

$$\mathsf{Up} : \Sigma\text{-}\mathbf{Alg}(\mathcal{C}) \cong \mathcal{C}^{\Sigma^*} : \mathsf{Dn}. \qquad (5.11)$$

We have already discussed one direction of the isomorphism. For the other direction, we need to extract a Σ-algebra from a Σ^*-algebra. The computation rules point in the right direction:

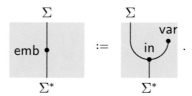

The calculation demonstrates that we can isolate the algebra underlying a fold if we precompose the latter with

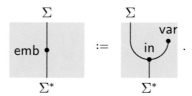

The natural transformation $\mathsf{emb} = \mathsf{in} \cdot \Sigma\circ\mathsf{var} : \Sigma \dot{\to} \Sigma^*$ turns a symbol into a singly layered term (a "flat" term), by placing variables in the argument positions. Notice the change of direction: to turn a Σ^*-algebra into a Σ-algebra, we make use of a natural transformation of type $\Sigma \dot{\to} \Sigma^*$. This is because the signature functor appears in a contravariant position in the action of an algebra.

To recap, the functors that witness the isomorphism (5.11) are defined as follows:

$$\mathsf{Up}\,(A, a : \Sigma\,A \to A) = (A, (\!(a)\!)) \qquad\qquad \mathsf{Up}\,h = h, \qquad (5.12a)$$

$$\mathsf{Dn}\,(B, b : \Sigma^{*}\,B \to B) = (B, b \cdot \mathsf{emb}\,B) \qquad\qquad \mathsf{Dn}\,h = h. \qquad (5.12b)$$

Observe that the functors are identities on arrows, so the functor laws are trivially satisfied. However, a number of proof obligations remain.

The functor Up maps a Σ-algebra to an algebra for the free monad Σ^{*}. We need to show that $(\!(a)\!)$ respects var and sub – this is (5.10b) and (5.10d) – and that Up maps Σ-homomorphisms to Σ^{*}-homomorphisms – this is the import of (5.10c).

Conversely, Dn maps an algebra for Σ^{*} to a Σ-algebra. It remains to show that Dn maps Σ^{*}-homomorphisms to Σ-homomorphisms. The proof is actually straightforward, merely applying the assumption that h is a Σ^{*}-homomorphism:

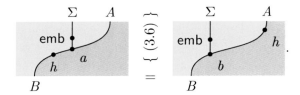

Since Dn preserves homomorphisms, the elevation rule (5.10c) can actually be strengthened to an equivalence.

Finally, we need to demonstrate that the functors are inverses. We have already established one direction: $\mathsf{Dn} \circ \mathsf{Up} = \mathsf{Id}$, using emb to extract the algebra underlying a fold. As an immediate consequence, we can express the free algebra in terms of the multiplication: $\mathsf{Dn}\,(\Sigma^{*}\,A, \mathsf{sub}\,A) = (\Sigma^{*}\,A, \mathsf{in}\,A)$, and consequently

$$\mathsf{in} = \mathsf{sub} \cdot \mathsf{emb} \circ \Sigma^{*}. \qquad (5.13)$$

For the other direction of the isomorphism, $\mathsf{Up} \circ \mathsf{Dn} = \mathsf{Id}$, we need to prove that $(\!(b \cdot \mathsf{emb}\,B)\!) = b$. We appeal to the universal property (5.9):

The Eilenberg–Moore unit axiom (3.8a) tells us that $b \cdot \mathsf{var}\,B = id$. It remains to show that the algebra $b : \Sigma^{*}\,B \to B$ is a Σ-homomorphism:

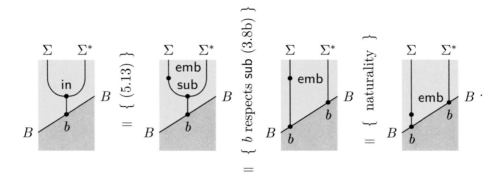

Consequently, the category of Eilenberg–Moore algebras of Σ^* is "the same thing" as the category of algebras of Σ. Intuitively, the monad Σ^* is free as it does not impose any further structure beyond that implied by the signature functor Σ.

5.3.3 Actions of a Free Monad. The free monad is also free in a more principled sense, as we shall explore from the perspective of actions in Section 5.3.4. As preparation, it is useful to extend the ideas of Section 5.3.2 from algebras to the actions of monads and endofunctors that were introduced in Section 3.6.

The free algebra (Σ^*, in) is an example of a vanilla action, with corresponding functor $\mathsf{Free}^\Sigma : \mathcal{C} \to \Sigma\text{-}\mathbf{Alg}(\mathcal{C})$. Furthermore, given a vanilla action α, the *natural* fold $(\!|\alpha|\!)$ with $(\!|\alpha|\!)\, A := (\!|\alpha\, A|\!)$ is a monad action for the free monad Σ^*:

$$\frac{\alpha : \Sigma \circ \mathsf{F} \dot\to \mathsf{F}}{(\!|\alpha|\!) : \Sigma^* \circ \mathsf{F} \dot\to \mathsf{F}}.$$

The requirements (3.10a) and (3.10b),

follow pointwise from Equations (5.10a) and (5.10d).

Remark 5.8. Now that we have seen that $(\!|\alpha|\!)$ yields a monad action from a vanilla action α, we can return to an important principle mentioned in Section 3.6. Relationships between endofunctor algebras and Eilenberg–Moore algebras can often be transferred to relationships between vanilla actions and monad actions, and vice versa.

In this case, a bit of thought shows that the computation rules (5.10a) and (5.10b), and the elevation rule (5.10c), lift from algebras to actions. In fact the functors Up and Dn introduced in Section 5.3.2 extend to actions, yielding an isomorphism between the categories of vanilla Σ-actions and Σ^*-actions, with their corresponding arrows.

We have already noted that the elevation rule (5.10c) can be strengthened to an equivalence, reflecting the fact that Up and Dn are identities on arrows. Instantiating h to the multiplication μ of some given monad in (5.10c), we obtain the following equivalence:

$$(5.14)$$

We can therefore restrict Up and Dn to an isomorphism between the full subcategories of M-*compatible vanilla* Σ-*actions* and M-*compatible* Σ^*-*actions*.

□

5.3.4 Free Monad of a Functor. A monad equips an endofunctor with additional structure, a unit and a multiplication. As with other algebraic structures, there is a forgetful functor,

$$U : \mathbf{Mnd}(\mathcal{C}) \to \mathcal{C}^{\mathcal{C}} \qquad \begin{aligned} U\,(M, \eta, \mu) &:= M, \\ U\,(\tau) &:= \tau, \end{aligned}$$

that forgets about the additional structure, sending a monad to its underlying endofunctor and a monad map to its underlying natural transformation.

We would like to find a left adjoint to U, and fortunately we have already done a lot of the work. Starting modestly, we fix a signature functor Σ, assuming that its free algebras exist. We have shown the following chain of bijections in previous sections:

$$\text{monad maps } \Sigma^* \to M$$
$$\cong \quad \{\ \text{Section 3.6, in particular (3.16)}\ \}$$
$$\text{M-compatible } \Sigma^*\text{-actions}$$
$$\cong \quad \{\ (5.11) \text{ and Remark 5.8}\ \}$$
$$\text{M-compatible vanilla } \Sigma\text{-actions}$$

$\cong$ { Section 3.6, in particular (3.16) }

natural transformations of type $\Sigma \to M$.

In the bottom-to-top direction, we have the following maps, where $(\!(\alpha)\!)$ is depicted by a rounded box drawn around the diagram for α.

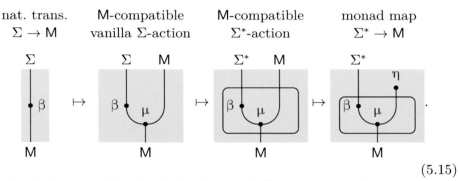

nat. trans.   M-compatible   M-compatible   monad map
$\Sigma \to M$ vanilla Σ-action Σ^*-action $\Sigma^* \to M$

$$(5.15)$$

The top-to-bottom direction is less involved. Precomposing the monad map with $\mathsf{emb} : \Sigma \dashrightarrow \Sigma^*$ does the trick.

monad map   M-compatible   M-compatible   nat. trans.
$\Sigma^* \to M$ Σ^*-action   vanilla Σ-action $\Sigma \to M$

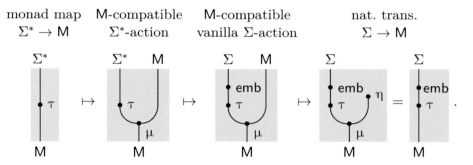

In other words, for each monad $M = (M, \eta, \mu)$ and for each natural transformation $\beta : \Sigma \dashrightarrow U M$, there exists a unique monad map $\tau : (\Sigma^*, \mathsf{var}, \mathsf{sub}) \to M$ such that $U\tau \cdot \mathsf{emb} = \beta$. This establishes that emb is a *universal arrow*!

If we assume that free algebras exist for *all* the endofunctors on our category, then emb is even a *universal transformation*. Invoking the machinery of Section 5.2, we conclude that the free algebra construction yields a left adjoint to the forgetful functor:

$$\mathbf{Mnd}(\mathcal{C}) \xleftarrow[\mathsf{U}]{\overset{\mathsf{Free}}{\underset{\perp}{\longleftarrow}}} \mathcal{C}^{\mathcal{C}} \qquad \begin{aligned} & \mathsf{Free}\,\Sigma = (\Sigma^*, \mathsf{var}, \mathsf{sub}), \\ & \mathsf{Free}\,\alpha = \alpha^*. \end{aligned} \tag{5.16}$$

For $\alpha : \Sigma_1 \dashrightarrow \Sigma_2$, we would like an explicit definition for the monad map $\alpha^* : \Sigma_1^* \to \Sigma_2^*$. Applying definition (5.5a), we evaluate the mapping (5.15) with

$\beta := \mathsf{emb}\,\Sigma_1 \cdot \alpha$, resulting in

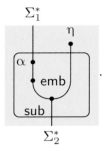

Symbolically, this is written as follows:

$$(\!|\mathsf{sub} \cdot (\mathsf{emb}\,\Sigma_1 \cdot \alpha) \circ \mathsf{M}|\!) \cdot (\Sigma^* \circ \eta).$$

Loosely speaking, the free monad $(\Sigma^*, \mathsf{var}, \mathsf{sub})$ is the most liberal structure that satisfies the monad axioms, which specialize to fundamental properties of substitution. As the elements of a free algebra are syntactic entities, first-order terms with variables, no further laws hold.

The reader may have noticed that we use the same notation for both the free monoid A^* and the free monad Σ^*. This is, of course, not a coincidence. From high in the sky, they are both instances of the same abstract concept: a standard monoid is a monoid in the category **Set**; a monad is a monoid in the category of endofunctors. It is a worthwhile enterprise to work through the details of the adjunction $\mathsf{Free} \dashv \mathsf{U} : \mathbf{Mnd}(\mathcal{C}) \to \mathcal{C}^{\mathcal{C}}$, relating the gadgets to their less mundane counterparts in the world of standard monoids.

The functorial action of Free on arrows, that is, natural transformations, implements a change of signature: given a signature changer $\alpha : \mathsf{F} \overset{.}{\to} \mathsf{G}$, the monad map $\alpha^* : \mathsf{F}^* \overset{.}{\to} \mathsf{G}^*$ translates F-terms into G-terms by applying α to each level of syntax. Recall: given an element changer $f : A \to B$, the monoid homomorphism $f^* : A^* \to B^*$, translates A-lists into B-lists by applying f to each element. (By contrast, fixing a signature Σ, the Σ-homomorphism $\Sigma^* f : \Sigma^* A \to \Sigma^* B$, renames variables in a given term by applying f to each variable.)

The unit of the adjunction is $\mathsf{emb}\,\Sigma : \Sigma \overset{.}{\to} \Sigma^*$, which is a higher-order natural transformation: it is natural in the signature Σ; each component $\mathsf{emb}\,\Sigma$ is itself a natural transformation. It turns a symbol into a singly layered term. Recall: *single* : $A \to A^*$ turns an element into a singleton list. (By contrast, $\mathsf{var}\,A : A \to \Sigma^* A$ turns a variable into a term.)

A component of the counit is a monad map of type $(\Sigma^*, \mathsf{var}, \mathsf{sub}) \to (\mathsf{M}, \eta, \mu)$. It reduces a term to an element of a monad using nested invocations of the multiplication: $(\!|\mu|\!) \cdot \mathsf{M}^* \circ \eta$. Recall: the monoid homomorphism *reduce* $(A, e, \bullet)$: $(A^*, [], +\!\!+) \to (A, e, \bullet)$ reduces a list to an element of a monoid using nested invocations of the multiplication. (By contrast, the fold $(\!(a)\!) :: \Sigma^* A \to A$ interprets a term, given an interpretation of symbols.)

Every adjunction induces a monad, and our adjunction is, of course, no exception: composing right and left adjoint yields the higher-order functor $(-)^*$ that maps an endofunctor Σ to the endofunctor Σ^*. To emphasize: Σ^* is a monad for a *fixed* signature Σ, and $(-)^*$ is a monad, as well. The former is induced by the free algebra construction (5.7), the latter by the free monad construction (5.16). Unit and multiplication of the monad $(-)^*$ are higher-order natural transformations with components

$$\Sigma \,\dot\to\, \Sigma^* \qquad \text{and} \qquad (\Sigma^*)^* \,\dot\to\, \Sigma^*.$$

The unit is, of course, emb, the unit of the adjunction. The multiplication flattens a term whose symbols are again terms into a single term. Recall: *join* $A : (A^*)^* \to A^*$ flattens a list whose elements are again lists into a single list. (By contrast, sub $A : \Sigma^* (\Sigma^* A) \to \Sigma^* A$ corresponds to substitution, flattening a term whose variables are again terms.)

To summarize, the following table overviews the gadgets of the three adjunctions we have just discussed.

	free algebra	free monad	free monoid
action of left adjoint	$\Sigma^* f$	α^*	f^*
unit	var	emb	*single*
counit	$(\!(a)\!)$	$(\!(\mu)\!) \cdot \mathsf{M}^* \circ \eta$	*reduce*
multiplication	sub	$(\!(\mu)\!) \cdot (\Sigma^*)^* \circ \eta$	*join*

If you feel adventurous, you may want to take things further, exploring the Kleisli and Eilenberg–Moore categories of the monad $(-)^*$.

Remark 5.9. We have been optimistic, in that we assumed that every endofunctor of type $\mathcal{C} \to \mathcal{C}$ has free algebras. Unfortunately, in most situations this is not the case, so the left adjoint to the forgetful functor will not exist at this level of generality.

Fortunately, all is not lost. The forgetful functor has a left adjoint if we restrict to a suitable class of endofunctors for which free algebras *do* exist, and is closed under the $(-)^*$ construction. Categories of endofunctors for which we can form free monads in this way do exist. For example, we could restrict to the polynomial functors on **Set**; these always have free algebras, and the resulting monads are also polynomial. If $\mathcal{C}$ is what is known as a locally presentable category, we can work with a much larger class of functors, the accessible functors, and all our constructions will work. The details would take us too far afield. Interested readers should see the standard reference (Adámek and Rosicky, 1994). ☐

5.4 The Resumption Monad

We now consider our final example, which involves much of what has gone before, including monads and adjunctions. We also take the opportunity to introduce another trick of the trade: the use of identity natural transformations in string diagrams. While this may seem against the overall spirit – the graphical notation encourages suppressing identity functors and natural transformations – you will shortly feel the benefit.

Let $M : \mathcal{C} \to \mathcal{C}$ be a monad and $F : \mathcal{C} \to \mathcal{C}$ be an endofunctor; we aim to show that $M \circ (F \circ M)^*$ is a monad. This construction is known as the *resumption monad* (Cenciarelli and Moggi, 1993), which plays an important role in concurrent programming.

As always, it is useful to generalize slightly: given a *right* monad action $\alpha : \Sigma \circ M \xrightarrow{\cdot} \Sigma$, we show that $M \circ \Sigma^*$ is a monad. To see that the resumption monad is an instance of the more general setup, set $\Sigma := F \circ M$ and $\alpha := F \circ \mu : (F \circ M) \circ M \xrightarrow{\cdot} (F \circ M)$. We already know that the multiplication μ is a right action (see Example 3.27) and that right actions are preserved by "outlining" the left edge (3.11) – Section 3.6 actually discusses left actions, but everything dualizes horizontally.

That we require an *action* is admittedly a bit of a rabbit. Alternatively, we could simply assume a vanilla action and discover during the proof that a proper action is needed.

Example 5.10. The maybe monad (see Example 3.5) is the simplest example of a free monad: $Maybe = K^*$, where K is the constant functor that sends every object to the terminal object: $K A = 1$; see also Exercise 5.12. Because of finality, there is a unique right action $K \circ M \xrightarrow{\cdot} K$, and we may conclude that $M \circ Maybe$ is a monad, as well. ☐

5.4.1 Huber at Work. We have got a monad M and furthermore an adjunction $Free^\Sigma \dashv U^\Sigma : \Sigma\text{-}\mathbf{Alg}(\mathcal{C}) \to \mathcal{C}$, so this sounds like an easy case for Huber. However, a moment's reflection reveals that the monad sits at the wrong end of the table:

$$\Sigma\text{-}\mathbf{Alg}(\mathcal{C}) \underset{U^\Sigma}{\overset{Free^\Sigma}{\rightleftarrows}} \mathcal{C} \circlearrowright M \, .$$

We need to move the monad (M, η, μ) to the left end, "lifting" it to the category of Σ-algebras and homomorphisms: $(\overline{M}, \overline{\eta}, \overline{\mu})$.

$$\overline{M} \left(\Sigma\text{-}\mathbf{Alg}(\mathcal{C}) \; \substack{\xrightarrow{\mathsf{Free}^\Sigma} \\ \bot \\ \xrightarrow[\mathsf{U}^\Sigma]{}} \; \mathcal{C} \right) M .$$

Lifting means that we get back the original monad, if we forget the additional structure, mapping an algebra to its carrier and a homomorphism to its underlying arrow:

$$\mathsf{U}^\Sigma \circ \overline{M} = M \circ \mathsf{U}^\Sigma, \tag{5.17a}$$
$$\mathsf{U}^\Sigma \circ \overline{\eta} = \eta \circ \mathsf{U}^\Sigma, \tag{5.17b}$$
$$\mathsf{U}^\Sigma \circ \overline{\mu} = \mu \circ \mathsf{U}^\Sigma. \tag{5.17c}$$

Assuming that we know how to equip the monad with the required structure, Huber's construction immediately yields the desired result:

$$\mathsf{U}^\Sigma \circ \overline{M} \circ \mathsf{Free}^\Sigma = M \circ \mathsf{U}^\Sigma \circ \mathsf{Free}^\Sigma = M \circ \Sigma^*.$$

Before we tackle the problem of lifting, let us pause for a moment to make unit η and multiplication μ of the composite monad more tangible. As a preparatory step, we draw the lifting conditions (5.17b) and (5.17c) as string diagrams (abbreviating U^Σ to U):

While the diagrams make plain the idea that unit and multiplication commute with the underlying functor, the diagrams are not entirely satisfactory. Rather irritatingly, the functor labels on the left-hand sides do not match the labels on the corresponding right-hand sides. For example, in the case of multiplication, the upper boundary reads $\mathsf{U}^\Sigma \circ \overline{M} \circ \overline{M}$ on the left and $M \circ M \circ \mathsf{U}^\Sigma$ on the right. Condition (5.17a) reassuringly tells us that both composites are equal, but this important piece of information is not included in the string diagram, which makes it hard to read in isolation. Fortunately, the problem can be readily resolved by adding explicit identity natural transformations,

$id : \mathsf{U}^\Sigma \circ \overline{\mathsf{M}} = \mathsf{M} \circ \mathsf{U}^\Sigma$, depicted as always by open circles:

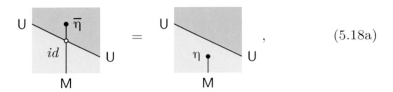

$$ (5.18a) $$

$$ (5.18b) $$

The drawings make the idea of traveling between worlds quite vivid, with the identities acting as windows. If the unit travels across, the window is closed, while the multiplication leaves two open windows behind. On a more technical note, the identities provide the valuable type information that was missing in the earlier diagrams. The identity $id : \mathsf{U}^\Sigma \circ \overline{\mathsf{M}} = \mathsf{M} \circ \mathsf{U}^\Sigma$ is somewhat unusual, as its source and target are not syntactically identical, but "only" equal. You may want to view it as a *type cast*.

We are now in a position to put the unit of the composite monad in concrete terms:

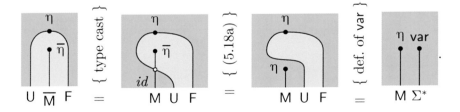

In the first step, we introduce an explicit type cast so that we can apply (5.18b). Perhaps unsurprisingly, we find that the unit of the composite is the horizontal composition of the units: $\eta = \eta \circ \mathsf{var}$. For the multiplication, we reason (abbreviating Free^{Σ} to Fr):

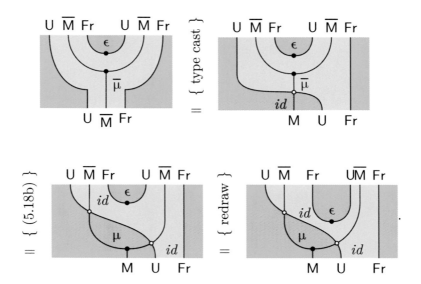

Again, in the first step we introduce an explicit type cast. Applying the scan line algorithm to the final diagram, we find that the composite multiplication is given by the vertical composition of M's multiplication and the counit, written as a fold (5.8) as follows:

$$\mu = \mu{\circ}\Sigma^* \cdot \mathsf{M}{\circ}(\![\overline{\mathsf{M}}\,(\Sigma^*, \mathsf{in})]\!),$$

where (Σ^*, in) is the natural free algebra. To determine the algebra of the fold, we have to flesh out the lifting $\overline{\mathsf{M}}$, which is what we do next.

5.4.2 Lifting a Monad. Property (5.17a) determines how $\overline{\mathsf{M}}$ acts on carriers and homomorphisms. So, we only have to think about the action part of an algebra. The following diagram illustrates what needs to be done:

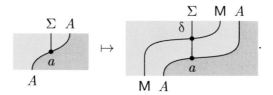

Roughly speaking, M is inserted between Σ and A. So, we need to fabricate a natural transformation of type $\Sigma{\circ}\mathsf{M} \overset{.}{\to} \mathsf{M}{\circ}\Sigma$. This is where the right monad action α comes into play:

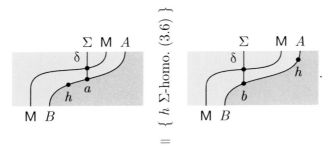

A lollipop serves as the missing leg – stretching metaphors a bit.

Now, since $\overline{\mathsf{M}}$ coincides with M on arrows, we know that it preserves identity and composition. It remains to show that $\overline{\mathsf{M}}$ also preserves Σ-homomorphisms. The proof is straightforward, merely applying the assumption that h is an Σ-homomorphism:

The homomorphism h freely operates "below" the functor M.

Finally, we need to determine the liftings of unit and multiplication. Fortunately, Properties (5.17b) and (5.17c) fully determine $\overline{\eta}$ and $\overline{\mu}$: $\overline{\eta}\,(A,\,a) = \eta\,A$ and $\overline{\mu}\,(A,\,a) = \mu\,A$. The liftings also satisfy the naturality properties and the monad laws. For example, $\overline{\eta}$'s naturality is shown as follows:

$$\overline{\mathsf{M}}\,h \cdot \overline{\eta}\,(A,\,a) = \overline{\eta}\,(B,\,b) \cdot h$$
$$\Longleftrightarrow \quad \{\ \mathsf{U}^{\Sigma}\ \text{faithful}\ \}$$
$$\mathsf{U}^{\Sigma}\,(\overline{\mathsf{M}}\,h \cdot \overline{\eta}\,(A,\,a)) = \mathsf{U}^{\Sigma}\,(\overline{\eta}\,(B,\,b) \cdot h)$$
$$\Longleftrightarrow \quad \{\ \mathsf{U}^{\Sigma}\ \text{functor (1.11b)}\ \}$$
$$\mathsf{U}^{\Sigma}\,(\overline{\mathsf{M}}\,h) \cdot \mathsf{U}^{\Sigma}\,(\overline{\eta}\,(A,\,a)) = \mathsf{U}^{\Sigma}\,(\overline{\eta}\,(B,\,b)) \cdot \mathsf{U}^{\Sigma}\,h$$
$$\Longleftrightarrow \quad \{\ \text{(5.17a) and (5.17b)}\ \}$$
$$\mathsf{M}\,(\mathsf{U}^{\Sigma}\,h) \cdot \eta\,(\mathsf{U}^{\Sigma}\,(A,\,a)) = \eta\,(\mathsf{U}^{\Sigma}\,(B,\,b)) \cdot \mathsf{U}^{\Sigma}\,h$$
$$\Longleftrightarrow \quad \{\ \text{definition of } \mathsf{U}^{\Sigma}\ \text{(5.6)}\ \}$$
$$\mathsf{M}\,(\mathsf{U}^{\Sigma}\,h) \cdot \eta\,A = \eta\,B \cdot \mathsf{U}^{\Sigma}\,h.$$

The final equality holds because η is natural.

It remains to prove that lifted unit and multiplication are natural homomorphisms. This is where the defining properties of a right action come into play. To show that each component of $\bar{\eta} : \mathsf{Id} \dot{\to} \overline{\mathsf{M}}$,

$$\bar{\eta}(A, a) : (A, a) \to (\mathsf{M}\, A, \mathsf{M}\, a \cdot \delta\, A),$$

is a homomorphism, we simply apply the unit action law:

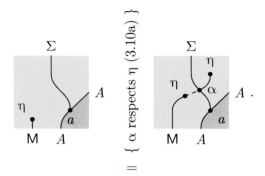

Likewise, to establish that each component of $\bar{\mu} : \overline{\mathsf{M}} \circ \overline{\mathsf{M}} \dot{\to} \overline{\mathsf{M}}$,

$$\bar{\mu}(A, a) : (\mathsf{M}\,(\mathsf{M}\, A), \mathsf{M}\,(\mathsf{M}\, a) \cdot \mathsf{M}\,(\delta\, A) \cdot \delta\,(\mathsf{M}\, A)) \to (\mathsf{M}\, A, \mathsf{M}\, a \cdot \delta\, A),$$

is a homomorphism, we reason

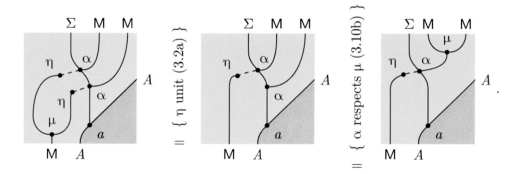

To the left of the functor Σ we apply the monad laws, and to its right the action laws. The broken staircase of η's and α's on the left is the diagrammatic rendering of $\mathsf{M}\,(\delta\, A) \cdot \delta\,(\mathsf{M}\, A)$.

We are now in a position to spell out the algebra $\overline{\mathsf{M}}\,(\Sigma^*, \mathsf{in})$, the missing piece in the definition of $\boldsymbol{\mu}$, the multiplication for the composite monad:

$$\overline{\mathsf{M}}\,(\Sigma^*, \mathsf{in}) = (\mathsf{M} \circ \Sigma^*, \mathsf{M} \circ \mathsf{in} \cdot \delta \circ \Sigma^*).$$

If we further unroll the definition of δ we obtain

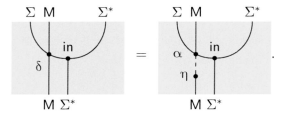

To summarize, unit and multiplication of our composite monad $T := M \circ \Sigma^*$ are defined:

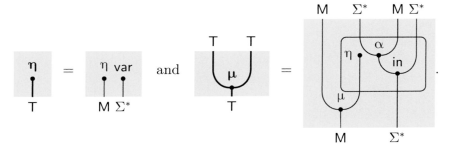

The diagrams bring together much of what we have discussed before: implosion and explosion of edges, boxing for universals, monads and monad actions, and, last but not least, free algebras and folds. They merit careful study.

Summary

An adjunction $L \dashv R$ defines both a monad $(R \circ L, \eta, R \circ \epsilon \circ L)$ and a comonad $(L \circ R, \epsilon, L \circ \eta \circ R)$.

A universal arrow from $A : \mathcal{D}$ to $R : \mathcal{C} \to \mathcal{D}$ consists of an object $L_A : \mathcal{C}$ and an arrow $\eta_A : A \to R L_A : \mathcal{D}$ such that the map

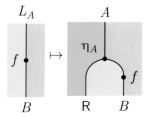

is a bijection between collections of arrows,

$$L_A \to B : \mathcal{C} \quad \cong \quad A \to R B : \mathcal{D},$$

that is natural in B. A universal transformation, a family of universal arrows, induces an adjunction.

The adjunction $\mathsf{Free}^\Sigma \dashv \mathsf{U}^\Sigma$ gives rise to the free monad $(\Sigma^*, \mathsf{var}, \mathsf{sub})$. The category of Σ-algebras is isomorphic to the Eilenberg–Moore category of the free monad Σ^*. The natural transformation

$$\mathsf{emb} = \mathsf{in} \cdot \Sigma \circ \mathsf{var} : \Sigma \stackrel{.}{\to} \mathsf{U}\,(\Sigma^*, \mathsf{var}, \mathsf{sub})$$

with $\mathsf{U} : \mathbf{Mnd}(\mathcal{C}) \to \mathcal{C}^\mathcal{C}$ is an example of a universal arrow.

Further Reading

Huber (1961) established that adjunctions induce monads. This raised the question of whether every monad arises in this way. Kleisli (1965) and Eilenberg and Moore (1965) provided two positive resolutions of this question, at opposite extremes. This topic will be explored in further detail in ESD.

The notion of monad makes sense in any bicategory (Bénabou, 1967), and much of "normal" monad theory involving categories, functors, and natural transformations can be extended to this setting, including analogues of the Kleisli and Eilenberg–Moore constructions (Street, 1995; Street and Lack, 2002; Vidal and Tur, 2010).

A diagrammatic account of adjunctions and their connection with monads is given in Hinze and Marsden (2016b). A delightful string diagrammatic approach to free monads appears in Piróg and Wu (2016).

We have used polynomial functors in various parts of this chapter. They have a very pleasant abstract theory, and their free monads are also polynomial (Gambino and Kock, 2013).

Exercises

5.1 ◯ Summarize the contents of this chapter in your own words.

5.2 ⊙ Given an adjunction $\mathsf{L} \dashv \mathsf{R}$, show that the composite

is an action for the monad $\mathsf{R} \circ \mathsf{L}$ induced by the adjunction.

5.3 ⊙ Recall that a semigroup is like a monoid, except that it need not have a unit. Show that the forgetful functor from monoids to semigroups that forgets about the unit element has a left adjoint. Which monad is induced by this adjunction?

5.4 ◉ Which comonads and monads are defined by the adjunctions of Exercise 4.4?

5.5 ⊙ Which comonads and monads are defined by the adjunctions of Exercise 4.5?

5.6 ◉ Apply Huber's construction to the composite adjunction L'∘L ⊣ R∘R'. Prove that if L' ⊣ R' yields the identity monad, then the composite adjunction defines the same monad as L ⊣ R. Can anything be said about the composite if L ⊣ R yields the identity monad?

5.7 ⊙ Continuing Exercise 3.7, show that an idempotent monad on $\mathcal{C}$ is equivalent to giving a reflective subcategory of $\mathcal{C}$. What can be said about the (co)monad induced by an equivalence of subcategories?

5.8 ⊙ Prove the following:

(a) If $(\Sigma, \epsilon, \delta)$ is a comonad, and $\iota : \Sigma \xrightarrow{\cdot} \mathsf{T}$ is an isomorphism, then T carries the structure of a comonad.

(b) For a pair of natural transformations $\delta, \epsilon : \mathsf{Id} \xrightarrow{\cdot} \mathsf{Id}$, they constitute a comonad on Id if and only if they are mutually inverse.

(c) Show that for adjunction L ⊣ R, if there exists *any* natural isomorphism $\iota : \mathsf{L}\circ\mathsf{R} \xrightarrow{\cdot} \mathsf{Id}$, then the counit of the adjunction is an isomorphism.

This is lemma 1.1.1 in Johnstone (2002a), but each part has a nice graphical interpretation.

5.9 ◉ Assume that we have an adjoint triple F ⊣ G ⊣ F. Show that the monad induced by the adjunction F ⊣ G together with the counit for G ⊣ F is Frobenius, see Exercises 4.20 and 4.22.

5.10 ⊙ The units of an adjunction can be defined in terms of the transpositions. Capture (4.4b) and (4.4e) graphically, using boxes for the transpositions.

5.11 ◉ Capture the properties of an adjunction graphically, using boxing. Extend the graphical calculus to include the units and formalize their interaction with boxing. Derive rules for bending the functor edge of a box.

5.12 ◉ Establish the following isomorphism:

$$\Sigma^* A \cong A + \Sigma\,(\Sigma^*\,A), \tag{5.19}$$

and conclude that Maybe $= \mathsf{K}^*$, where K is the constant functor that sends every object to the terminal object: $\mathsf{K}\,A = 1$.

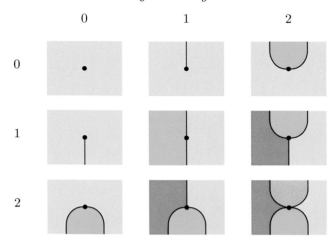

Figure 5.2 Gadgets with m arms and n legs $(0 \leqslant m, n \leqslant 2)$.

5.13 ⊙ Show that the following statements are all *false* – the analogy to regular algebra should not be taken too far:

$$F^* \circ F^* \cong F^*, \tag{5.20a}$$
$$(F^*)^* \cong F^*, \tag{5.20b}$$
$$F \circ (G \circ F)^* \cong (F \circ G)^* \circ F, \tag{5.20c}$$
$$F^* \circ (G \circ F^*)^* \cong (F + G)^* \cong G^* \circ (F \circ G^*)^*. \tag{5.20d}$$

5.14 ⊙ Figure 5.2 lists all types of natural transformations with m arms and n legs $(0 \leqslant m, n \leqslant 2)$. Browse through the monograph to find examples for each type of gadget.

Epilogue

As we have seen, string diagrams transform category theory into a beautiful, visual subject. We hope that we have whetted your appetite for more. Readers looking to further deepen their knowledge of string diagrams may wish to seek out the forthcoming book "Exploring String Diagrams," where we shall push further into the world of diagrammatic reasoning:

- Chapter 1 continues to explore universals, looking at the concept from several angles. Along the way it introduces one of the most important results of category theory, the Yoneda lemma.
- Chapter 2 looks at an important example of universals, limits and colimits, and their interaction with adjunctions.
- We have already encountered the Eilenberg–Moore and Kleisli categories associated with a monad. Chapter 3 will take this investigation further. This will including sharpening the relationship between adjunctions and monads, and showing how structure such as functors and natural transformations can be lifted to Eilenberg–Moore and Kleisli categories.
- Chapter 4 continues the study of monads, from the perspective of compositionality. We look at how monads can be combined together, and the structure of composite monads.
- Adjunctions also have rich compositional structure, and this will be the focus of Chapter 5. This will involve a wide generalization of the notion of mates we saw in Chapter 4, and again the idea of lifting structure to Kleisli and Eilenberg–Moore categories will be significant.
- Finally, the important topic of Kan extensions will be covered in Chapter 6. We will find that Kan extensions connect with almost everything we have seen before: adjunctions, monads, universal objects, and limits and colimits.

Along the way, we will find many additional applications of our newfound artistic skills, and see how more advanced and powerful categorical techniques can be understood diagrammatically. We will also encounter new tricks and relationships as we delve further into the realm of string diagrams.

Appendix

Notation

This section contains references to notation that was introduced throughout the book. Some additional notation is defined here for the convenience of the reader.

Meta Variables ───

$\mathcal{C}$, $\mathcal{D}$ ...	categories	1
A, B ...	objects	1
f, g ...	arrows	1
F, G ...	functors	13
α, β ...	natural transformations	18
$\mathbb{B}$, $\mathbb{Z}$ ...	the type of Booleans, the type of integers, ...	–

Notation ───

:=	definitional equality: in $x := e$ the entity on the left is defined in terms of the entity on the right	–
=:	definitional equality: in $e =: x$ the entity on the right is defined in terms of the entity on the left	–
$f\,x$	function application	–
$a \times -$	partially applying the binary operator "$\times$" to the first argument	–
$- \times b$	partially applying the binary operator "$\times$" to the second argument	–
$- \times =$	the binary operator "$\times$" viewed as a function	–
A^*	the set of all finite lists, whose elements are drawn from A (Kleene star)	16
$\mathcal{P}\,A$	the set of all sets, whose elements are drawn from A (powerset)	–

Constructions

Categories

Ab	the category of Abelian groups and their homomorphisms	110
Bool	the category of Boolean lattices and their homomorphisms	3
CMon	the category of commutative monoids and monoid homomorphisms	4
CIMon	the category of commutative, idempotent monoids and monoid homomorphisms	4
CompLat	the category of complete lattices and monotone maps that preserve arbitrary joins and meets	3
Fin	the category of finite sets and total functions	4
Mon	the category of monoids and monoid homomorphisms	3
Poset	the category of partial orders and monotone functions	126
Pre	the category of preorders and monotone functions	3
Reg	the category of regular algebras (aka quantales) and join-preserving monoid homomorphism	102
Rel	the category of sets and relations	2
Ring	the category of rings and their homomorphisms	126
Set	the category of sets and total functions	2
Sup	the category of complete join-semilattices and monotone maps that preserve arbitrary joins	3

Functors

$2^{(-)}$	contravariant powerset functor	15
Bag	the finite bag functor (bags are also known as multisets)	66
List	the finite list functor	16
Pow	covariant powerset functor	14
Set	the finite set functor	2

Cheat Sheet

Basic Diagrams

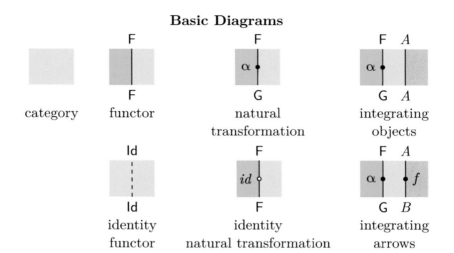

| category | functor | natural transformation | integrating objects |

| identity functor | identity natural transformation | integrating arrows |

Monads M : $\mathcal{C} \to \mathcal{C}$

$$M : \mathcal{C} \to \mathcal{C}$$
$$\eta : \mathsf{Id} \dot{\to} M$$
$$\mu : M{\circ}M \dot{\to} M$$

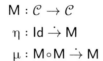

Categories of Algebras F-Alg($\mathcal{C}$)

algebra (A, a) homomorphism $h : (A, a) \to (B, b)$

Adjunctions L ⊣ R : $\mathcal{C} \to \mathcal{D}$

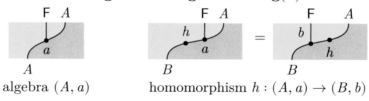

$$\mathcal{C} \; \underset{R}{\overset{L}{\rightleftarrows}} \; \mathcal{D}$$

$$\mathsf{L}\, A \to B \cong A \to \mathsf{R}\, B$$

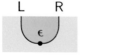

Cheat Sheet

Free Algebras Free$^\Sigma$ $\dashv$ U$^\Sigma$: Σ-**Alg**$(\mathcal{C})$ $\rightharpoonup$ $\mathcal{C}$

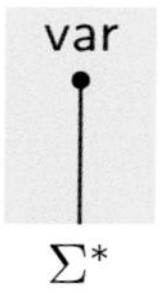

Σ $\quad$ Σ^*	Σ^* $\quad$ A

$$\text{var}$$

$$\Sigma^*$$

unit

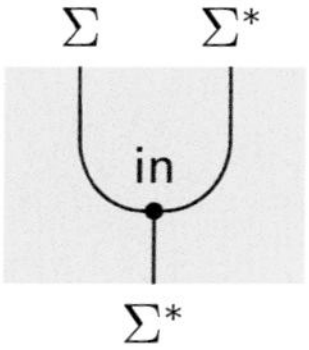

$$\text{in}$$

$$\Sigma^*$$

free algebra

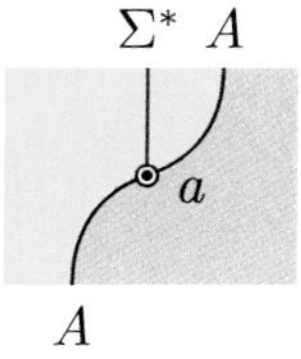

$$a$$

$$A$$

fold $(\!(a)\!)$

Diagrammatic Moves

sliding

$$\text{F} \quad X$$
$$\alpha X$$
$$h$$
$$\text{G} \quad Y$$

$\mapsto$

$$\text{F} \quad X$$
$$h$$
$$\alpha Y$$
$$\text{G} \quad Y$$

bending

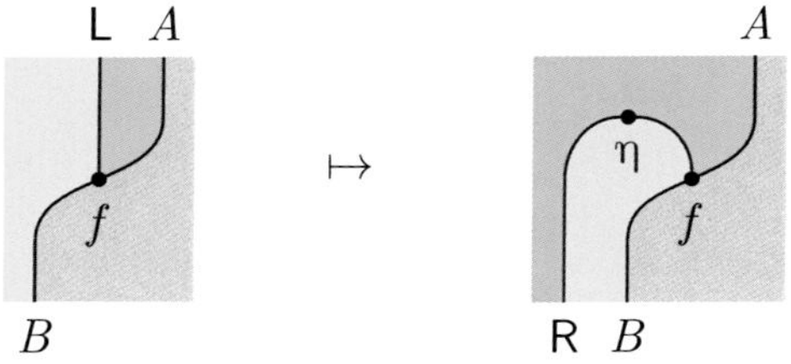

$$\text{L} \quad A$$
$$f$$
$$B$$

$\mapsto$

$$A$$
$$\eta$$
$$f$$
$$\text{R} \quad B$$

boxing

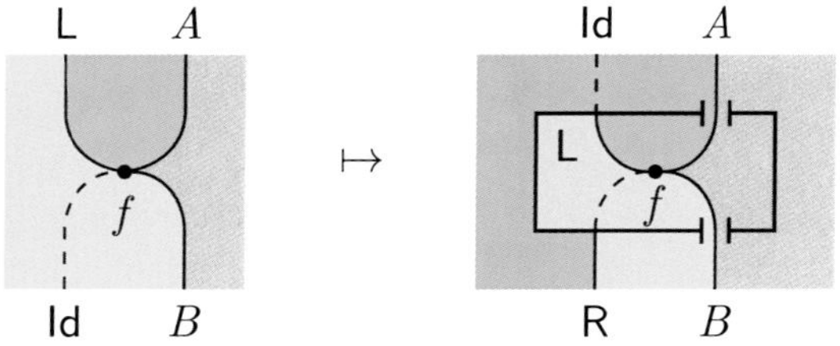

$$\text{L} \qquad A$$
$$f$$
$$\text{Id} \quad B$$

$\mapsto$

$$\text{Id} \quad A$$
$$\text{L}$$
$$f$$
$$\text{R} \quad B$$

References

Abramsky, S., and Coecke, B. 2004. A categorical semantics of quantum protocols. Pages 415–425 of: *19th IEEE Symposium on Logic in Computer Science (LICS 2004), 14-17 July 2004, Turku, Finland, Proceedings.* Institute of Electrical and Electronic Engineers. https://doi.org/10.1109/LICS.2004.1319636. (Cited on Page xi.)

Adámek, J., and Rosicky, J. 1994. *Locally Presentable and Accessible Categories.* London Mathematical Society Lecture Notes Series, vol. 189. Cambridge University Press. (Cited on Page 157.)

Awodey, S. 2010. *Category Theory.* Oxford Logic Guides, vol. 52. Oxford University Press. (Cited on Page 27.)

Backhouse, R. 1989. Making formality work for us. *EATCS Bulletin,* **38**(June), 219–249. (Cited on Pages x and 56.)

Backhouse, R., Bijsterveld, M., van Geldrop, R., and Van Der Woude, J. 1998. *Category theory as coherently constructive lattice theory.* Computer Science Reports 9443. Eindhoven University of Technology. (Cited on Pages 20 and 27.)

Baez, J. C., and Erbele, J. 2015. Categories in control. *Theory and Applications of Categories,* **30**(24), 836–881. (Cited on Pages xii and 55.)

Baez, J. C., and Fong, B. 2015. A compositional framework for passive linear networks. *arXiv:1504.05625.* (Cited on Pages xii and 55.)

Baez, J. C., Fong, B., and Pollard, B. S. 2016. A compositional framework for Markov processes. *Journal of Mathematical Physics,* **57**(3). (Cited on Pages xii and 55.)

Barr, M., and Wells, C. 2005. Toposes, triples and theories. *Reprints in Theory and Applications of Categories,* **12**, 1–287. (Cited on Page 87.)

Bénabou, J. 1967. *Introduction to Bicategories.* Lecture Notes in Mathematics, vol. 47. Springer. (Cited on Pages 33, 55, 63, and 164.)

Bonchi, F., Sobocinski, P., and Zanasi, F. 2015. Full abstraction for signal flow graphs. *ACM SIGPLAN Notices,* **50**(1), 515–526. (Cited on Pages xii and 55.)

Borceux, F. 1994a. *Handbook of Categorical Algebra: Volume 1, Basic Category Theory.* Encyclopedia of Mathematics and Its Applications, vol. 50. Cambridge University Press. (Cited on Page 27.)

Borceux, F. 1994b. *Handbook of Categorical Algebra: Volume 2, Categories and*

Structures. Encyclopedia of Mathematics and Its Applications, vol. 51. Cambridge University Press. (Cited on Page 27.)

Borceux, F. 1994c. *Handbook of Categorical Algebra: Volume 3, Sheaf Theory*. Encyclopedia of Mathematics and Its Applications, vol. 52. Cambridge University Press. (Cited on Page 27.)

Brown, C., and Hutton, G. 1994. Categories, allegories and circuit design. Pages 372–381 of: *Proceedings of the Ninth Annual Symposium on Logic in Computer Science (LICS '94), Paris, France, July 4-7, 1994*. Institute of Electrical and Electronic Engineers. `https://doi.org/10.1109/LICS.1994.316052`. (Cited on Pages xii and 55.)

Cenciarelli, P., and Moggi, E. 1993. A syntactic approach to modularity in denotational semantics. In: *Category Theory and Computer Science*. `https://person.dibris.unige.it/moggi-eugenio/ftp/mod-sem.pdf`. (Cited on Page 157.)

Cheng, E. 2011. Iterated distributive laws. *Mathematical Proceedings of the Cambridge Philosophical Society*, **150**(3), 459–487. (Cited on Page 48.)

Coecke, B., and Kissinger, A. 2017. *Picturing Quantum Processes*. Cambridge University Press. (Cited on Pages xii and 55.)

Coecke, B., Sadrzadeh, M., and Clark, S. 2010. Mathematical foundations for distributed compositional models of meaning. Lambek Festschrift. *Linguistic Analysis*, **36**(1-4), 345–384. (Cited on Pages xii and 55.)

Crole, R. L. 1993. *Categories for Types*. Cambridge University Press. (Cited on Page 27.)

Curien, P.-L. 2008a. Category theory: A programming language-oriented introduction. *Forthcoming book based on lecture notes*. `https://www.irif.fr/~mellies/mpri/mpri-ens/articles/curien-category-theory.pdf`. (Cited on Page x.)

Curien, P. L. 2008b. The Joy of String Diagrams. Pages 15–22 of: *Computer Science Logic, 22nd International Workshop, CSL 2008, 17th Annual Conference of the EACSL, Bertinoro, Italy, September 16-19, 2008. Proceedings*. Lecture Notes in Computer Science, vol. 5213. Springer. (Cited on Pages x and 55.)

Davey, B. A., and Priestley, H. A. 2002. *Introduction to Lattices and Order*. Cambridge University Press. (Cited on Pages 27 and 67.)

Dubuc, E. J., and Szyld, M. 2013. A Tannakian context for Galois theory. *Advances in Mathematics*, **234**, 528–549. `https://www.sciencedirect.com/science/article/pii/S0001870812004094`. (Cited on Page 38.)

Eilenberg, S., and MacLane, S. 1945. General theory of natural equivalences. *Transactions of the American Mathematical Society*, **58**(2), 231–294. `http://www.jstor.org/stable/1990284`. (Cited on Page 27.)

Eilenberg, S., and Moore, J. C. 1965. Adjoint functors and triples. *Illinois Journal of Math*, **9**(3), 381–398. (Cited on Pages 63, 73, 87, and 164.)

Fokkinga, M. M. 1992a. *A Gentle Introduction to Category Theory – The Calculational Approach*. Vol. Part I. University of Utrecht. Pages 1–72. (Cited on Page 56.)

Fokkinga, M. M. 1992b. Calculate categorically! *Formal Aspects of Computing*, **4**(4), 673–692. (Cited on Page 56.)

Fokkinga, M. M., and Meertens, L. 1994 (June). *Adjunctions*. Tech. rept. Memoranda Informatica 94-31. University of Twente. (Cited on Pages ix and 56.)

Fong, B., Spivak, D. I., and Tuyéras, R. 2019. Backprop as functor: A compositional perspective on supervised learning. Pages 1–13 of: *34th Annual*

ACM/IEEE Symposium on Logic in Computer Science, LICS 2019, Vancouver, BC, Canada, June 24-27, 2019. Institute of Electrical and Electronic Engineers. https://doi.org/10.1109/LICS.2019.8785665. (Cited on Page xii.)

Gambino, N., and Kock, J. 2013. Polynomial functors and polynomial monads. Pages 153–192 of: *Mathematical Proceedings of the Cambridge Philosophical Society*, vol. 154. Cambridge University Press. (Cited on Page 164.)

Gasteren, van, A. J. M. 1988. *On the shape of mathematical arguments.* Ph.D. thesis, Department of Mathematics and Computer Science. (Cited on Page 23.)

Ghani, N., Hedges, J., Winschel, V., and Zahn, P. 2018a. Compositional game theory. Pages 472–481 of: *Proceedings of the 33rd Annual ACM/IEEE Symposium on Logic in Computer Science, LICS 2018, Oxford, UK, July 09-12, 2018.* Association for Computing Machinery. https://doi.org/10.1145/3209108.3209165. (Cited on Page xii.)

Ghani, N., Kupke, C., Lambert, A., and Nordvall Forsberg, F. 2018b. A compositional treatment of iterated open games. *Theoretical Computer Science*, **741**, 48–57. Part of special issue An Observant Mind : Essays Dedicated to Don Sannella on the Occasion of his 60th Birthday. (Cited on Page xii.)

Ghica, D. R., and Jung, A. 2016. Categorical semantics of digital circuits. Pages 41–48 of: *2016 Formal Methods in Computer-Aided Design, FMCAD 2016, Mountain View, CA, USA, October 3-6, 2016.* Institute of Electrical and Electronic Engineers. https://doi.org/10.1109/FMCAD.2016.7886659. (Cited on Pages xii and 55.)

Gibbons, J., Henglein, F., Hinze, R., and Wu, N. 2018. Relational algebra by way of adjunctions. *Proceedings of the ACM on Programming Languages*, **2**(ICFP), Article 86: pp. 1–28. https://doi.org/10.1145/3236781. (Cited on Page 123.)

Godement, R. 1964. *Théorie des faisceaux.* Hermann. (Cited on Pages 63 and 87.)

Gries, D., and Schneider, F. B. 2013. *A Logical Approach to Discrete Math.* Monographs in Computer Science. Springer. (Cited on Page x.)

Heunen, C., and Vicary, J. 2019. *Categories for Quantum Theory: An Introduction.* Oxford University Press. (Cited on Page xii.)

Hinze, R. 2012. Kan extensions for program optimisation or: Art and Dan explain an old trick. Pages 324–362 of: *Mathematics of Program Construction - 11th International Conference, MPC 2012, Madrid, Spain, June 25-27, 2012. Proceedings.* Lecture Notes in Computer Science, vol. 7342. Springer. https://doi.org/10.1007/978-3-642-31113-0_16. (Cited on Page xii.)

Hinze, R. 2013. Adjoint folds and unfolds – An extended study. *Science of Computer Programming*, **78**(11), 2108–2159. (Cited on Page 123.)

Hinze, R., and Marsden, D. 2016a. Dragging proofs out of pictures. Pages 152–168 of: *A List of Successes That Can Change the World: Essays Dedicated to Philip Wadler on the Occasion of His 60th Birthday.* Springer. http://dx.doi.org/10.1007/978-3-319-30936-1_8. (Cited on Pages xii, 55, and 88.)

Hinze, R., and Marsden, D. 2016b. Equational reasoning with lollipops, forks, cups, caps, snakes, and speedometers. *Journal of Logical and Algebraic Methods in Programming*, **85**(5), 931–951. http://dx.doi.org/10.1016/j.jlamp.2015.12.004. (Cited on Pages xii, 55, and 164.)

Hinze, R., and Wu, N. 2016. Unifying structured recursion schemes: an extended study. *Journal of Functional Programming*, **26**. (Cited on Page 123.)

Hinze, R., Wu, N., and Gibbons, J. 2013. Unifying structured recursion schemes. Pages 209–220 of: *Proceedings of the 18th ACM SIGPLAN International Conference on Functional Programming*. ICFP '13. Association for Computing Machinery. http://doi.acm.org/10.1145/2500365.2500578. (Cited on Page 123.)

Huber, P. J. 1961. Homotopy theory in general categories. *Mathematische Annalen*, **144**, 361–385. http://dx.doi.org/10.1007/BF01396534. (Cited on Pages 129 and 164.)

Johnstone, P. T. 2002a. *Sketches of an Elephant: A Topos Theory Compendium Volume 1*. Oxford Logic Guides, vol. 43. Oxford University Press. (Cited on Pages 27 and 165.)

Johnstone, P. T. 2002b. *Sketches of an Elephant: A Topos Theory Compendium Volume 2*. Oxford Logic Guides, vol. 44. Oxford University Press. (Cited on Page 27.)

Joyal, A., and Street, R. 1998. *Planar diagrams and tensor algebra*. Unpublished manuscript, available from Ross Street's website. (Cited on Page 55.)

Joyal, André, and Street, Ross. 1991. The geometry of tensor calculus, I. *Advances in Mathematics*, **88**(1), 55–112. http://www.sciencedirect.com/science/article/pii/000187089190003P. (Cited on Pages 43 and 55.)

Kan, D. M. 1958. Adjoint functors. *Transactions of the American Mathematical Society*, **87**(2), 294–329. (Cited on Pages 91 and 123.)

Kleisli, H. 1965. Every standard construction is induced by a pair of adjoint functors. *Proceedings of the American Mathematical Society*, **16**(3), 544–546. http://www.jstor.org/stable/2034693. (Cited on Pages 73, 87, 89, and 164.)

Leinster, T. 2014. *Basic Category Theory*. Cambridge Studies in Advanced Mathematics, vol. 143. Cambridge University Press. (Cited on Pages x and 27.)

Mac Lane, S. 1998. *Categories for the Working Mathematician*. 2nd edn. Graduate Texts in Mathematics. Springer. (Cited on Pages ix, 1, 13, 27, 63, and 91.)

Manes, E. G. 1976. *Algebraic Theories*. Graduate Texts in Mathematics. Springer. (Cited on Page 63.)

Marsden, D. 2014. Category theory using string diagrams. **abs/1401.7220**. http://arxiv.org/abs/1401.7220. (Cited on Page xii.)

Marsden, D. 2015. *Logical aspects of quantum computation*. Ph.D. thesis, University of Oxford. http://ora.ox.ac.uk/objects/uuid:e99331a3-9d93-4381-8075-ad843fb9b77c. (Cited on Pages xii and 55.)

Melliès, P.-A. 2006. Functorial Boxes in String Diagrams. Pages 1–30 of: *Computer Science Logic, 20th International Workshop, CSL 2006, 15th Annual Conference of the EACSL, Szeged, Hungary, September 25-29, 2006, Proceedings*. Lecture Notes in Computer Science, vol. 4207. Springer. https://doi.org/10.1007/11874683_1. (Cited on Page 55.)

Melliès, P.-A. 2012. Game Semantics in String Diagrams. Pages 481–490 of: *Proceedings of the 27th Annual IEEE Symposium on Logic in Computer Science, LICS 2012, Dubrovnik, Croatia, June 25-28, 2012*. IEEE Computer Society. https://doi.org/10.1109/LICS.2012.58. (Cited on Page 55.)

Moggi, E. 1991. Notions of computation and monads. *Information and Computation*, **93**(1), 55–92. (Cited on Page 87.)

Penrose, R. 1971. Applications of negative dimensional tensors. Pages 221–244 of: *Combinatorial Mathematics and Its Applications: Proceedings of a Conference held at the Mathematical Institute, Oxford, from 7–10 July, 1969.* Academic Press. (Cited on Page ix.)

Piróg, M., and Wu, N. 2016. String diagrams for free monads (functional pearl). Pages 490–501 of: *Proceedings of the 21st ACM SIGPLAN International Conference on Functional Programming, ICFP 2016, Nara, Japan, September 18-22, 2016.* Association for Computing Machinery. `https://doi.org/10.1145/2951913.2951947`. (Cited on Page 164.)

Piróg, M., Wu, N., and Gibbons, J. 2015. Modules over monads and their algebras. Pages 290–303 of: *6th Conference on Algebra and Coalgebra in Computer Science, CALCO 2015, June 24-26, 2015, Nijmegen, The Netherlands.* LIPIcs, vol. 35. Schloss Dagstuhl – Leibniz-Zentrum für Informatik. `https://doi.org/10.4230/LIPIcs.CALCO.2015.290`. (Cited on Page 88.)

Selinger, P. 2011. A survey of graphical languages for monoidal categories. Pages 289–355 of: Coecke, B. (ed), *New Structures for Physics.* Lecture Notes in Physics, vol. 813. Springer. (Cited on Page 55.)

Sobocinski, P. 2019. *Graphical Linear Algebra.* Mathematical blog, accessed December 18th 2022 from https://graphicallinearalgebra.net/. (Cited on Pages xii and 55.)

Spivak, D. I. 2014. *Category Theory for the Sciences.* Massachusetts Institute of Technology Press. (Cited on Page 27.)

Stone, M. H. 1936. The theory of representation for Boolean algebras. *Transactions of the American Mathematical Society,* **40**(1), 37–111. (Cited on Page 112.)

Stone, M. H. 1937. Applications of the theory of Boolean rings to general topology. *Transactions of the American Mathematical Society,* **41**(3), 375–481. (Cited on Page 112.)

Street, R. 1995. Low-dimensional topology and higher-order categories. In: *Proceedings of CT95.* `http://science.mq.edu.au/~street/LowDTop.pdf`. (Cited on Pages 55, 57, and 164.)

Street, R. 1996. Categorical structures. *Handbook of Algebra,* **1**, 529–577. (Cited on Pages 33 and 56.)

Street, R., and Lack, S. 2002. The formal theory of monads II. *Journal of Pure and Applied Algebra,* **175**(1), 243–265. (Cited on Page 164.)

Vidal, J. B. C., and Tur, J. C. S. 2010. Kleisli and Eilenberg–Moore constructions as parts of biadjoint situations. *Extracta Mathematicae,* **25**(1), 1–61. (Cited on Page 164.)

Wadler, P. 1989. Theorems for free! Pages 347–359 of: *Proceedings of the Fourth International Conference on Functional Programming Languages and Computer Architecture.* Association for Computing Machinery. `http://doi.acm.org/10.1145/99370.99404`. (Cited on Page 27.)

Wadler, P. 1995. Monads for functional programming. Pages 24–52 of: Jeuring, J., and Meijer, E. (eds), *Advanced Functional Programming, First International Spring School on Advanced Functional Programming Techniques, Båstad, Sweden, May 24-30, 1995, Tutorial Text.* Lecture Notes in Computer Science, vol. 925. Springer. `https://doi.org/10.1007/3-540-59451-5_2`. (Cited on Page 87.)

Index